Containers

Containers

Essential know-how and expert advice for gardening success

CONTENTS

Container gardening brings texture and color right up to the home, on patios, pathways, and paving. It is simple to make changes and easy to be creative, without fear of getting it wrong—the results can be spectacular.

PLANNING, PLANTING, AND GROWING

Whatever your vision—perhaps a cottage-style garden, with a mix of colorful flowers, or a minimalist design with more angular shapes—with good planning, it is quite simple to create a container garden that will thrive and look great.

PROBLEM-FREE GARDENING

Growing your favorite plants in pots eliminates many of the usual problems facing gardeners. First, you will start off with clean potting mix—and therefore without the problem of weeds. Your plants should also be pest- and disease-free, initially at least. And because you can fill pots with mix to suit the needs of your chosen plants, you will not have to fight to keep them alive. Whether your garden soil is too dry or too wet, too heavy or sandy, is irrelevant—growing plants in containers means you can create and control the ideal conditions.

REFLECTING YOUR STYLE

Whether you live in an ultra-modern apartment with a balcony in the heart of the city or in a country cottage, surrounded by trees and hedges, you can plan your container garden to reflect your style. Whenever you want to use your outdoor space, it can be packed with color and interest, using plants that thrive in the height of summer or the depths of winter. And changing the look is easy: with the exception of your largest pots, you can move plants around, adding pots of color, or removing them when plants stop blooming or when you want a change.

GARDENS FOR ALL AGES

Whether you are young or not so young, container gardening is likely to be perfect for you. There is no heavy digging, very few weeds to tackle, and plants are raised up off the ground, making them easy to look after and appreciate. Almost anything can be grown in a pot, so there is no need to miss out on raising your favorite flowers—and all those fragrant blooms that are often so close to the ground will be within easy sniffing distance. New gardeners, both the young and more mature, will love creating their own small garden in a pot, choosing their plants, caring for them, and seeing them thrive. Because container plants are protected from many threats and receive constant attention, they are far more likely to flourish than if in the open garden. With success virtually guaranteed, new gardeners are likely to become lifelong gardeners.

THE APPEAL OF CONTAINER GARDENING

Growing plants in containers is creative, fun, and accessible. It also offers great flexibility: you can group plants that may not grow well together in a garden, combine several plants in one pot, and even change your displays according to the season and your mood so that they always look fresh. Results can be instant, yet you can also nurture trees and shrubs for many years to come.

Cosmos and salvia team with other flowers in an informal, staggered display.

Using the right potting mix for more picky plants is often the key to success.

TAILORING POTTING MIX

Part of the appeal of containers is that you can grow fussier plants in more specialized soil than if you were planting them in your backyard. For example, camellias, rhododendrons, and pieris need lime-free (ericaceous) soil, while shrubs and trees are happiest in enriched versions. Some alpine plants need perfect drainage, which is easily provided if grown in shallow troughs or pots: use an enriched potting mix with some grit to improve drainage. Pots of moisture-loving ferns grow to perfection on a shady patio: add a little extra organic matter to multipurpose mix to help it retain moisture.

GROWING TENDER PLANTS

Plants that are unable to stand severe frost, or a combination of cold and wet, are perfect for pots because they can be protected in winter. Tender plants include some of the most dramatic and colorful plants available for summer display, such as begonias, fuchsias, pelargoniums, and dahlias. Readily available, you can treat these plants as annuals and enjoy them for one year or, with care, save them for another season.

Tender bulbs and plants that lose their leaves can be stored in a garage, if they are kept moist. Evergreens can be put in a cold greenhouse or even placed against the house, where it is more sheltered, until spring arrives. Cannas, bananas, and aeonium will give your pots a tropical look and quickly transform a mediocre display into something really striking. Some houseplants, such as spider plants and succulents, grow well outside during the summer months and will add a luxuriant feel to your patio display.

Fuchsias can be stored safely in a greenhouse throughout the winter months.

The red-tinged leaves of the Abyssinian banana bring drama to any arrangement.

STYLING YOUR SPACE

Plants and containers come in a wide range of sizes, shapes, textures, and colors. The successful interplay between these different elements lies at the heart of container gardening and can transform a mundane space into a visual feast. Use these features to theme your display and highlight your pots and plants. This is your chance to get really creative.

Tall pots, including old chimney pots, lift low, arching plants such as grasses, while round pots offset large-leaved plants like hostas. Wooden tubs suit shade-loving pieris, acers, and rhododendrons; metal containers enhance silvery succulents.

Containers can also inject color and drama into your garden or patio by complementing or contrasting with your plants: black pots, for example, show off blue and white flowers; blue pots contrast with yellow flowers. A simple planting of bright violas or daffodils and yellow foliage, such as choisya or hostas, look wonderful in rich blue pots. The containers you choose will also help create the overall mood you are aiming for—terra-cotta will age with time, while glazed pots will retain a shiny, fresh look.

Create a rustic look with wicker and ceramic pots in different shapes and sizes.

GARDENING WITHOUT A GARDEN

Containers allow you to create a garden even if you do not have access to garden soil. Arrange pots on windowsills, balconies, low walls, and patios. A simple pot of flowers or a bay or palm plant will soften and enliven a severe patio area. Place small pots of flowers at the edge of steps to introduce sparkle and interest. Break up walls or fences with pots of tall plants or hang baskets and fix troughs to bring vibrant color into an otherwise dull space.

Artfully positioned container plants can create a vibrant yet intimate seating area.

PLANNING A GROUPED DISPLAY

Container gardening allows you the freedom to arrange and rearrange your pots as the mood strikes you: grouping plants together for impact or for their similar habits and needs; or even contrasting different types and colors of plants for maximum visual effect. You can buy plants in flower to add to your groupings and experiment with your displays in different areas of your garden or patio. Above all, you can be creative.

Restricting your color palette can be effective, as in this mix of vibrant dahlias, golden bidens, and fiery marigolds.

Hostas are great for pots, with huge variation in leaf shape, color, and size.

GROUPING SIMILAR-LOOKING PLANTS

Grouping plants that are visually similar often brings calm and cohesion to a display, but it can also emphasize subtle differences. Succulents, for example, look great grouped together (see p.32) and hostas are also ideal in this respect: they are similar in form (and most like similar conditions), but have sufficient contrast in color and size to create a tranquil but impressive display. Highlight differences in flower shape, size, and texture with monochromatic groupings of yellow or gray foliage, white flowers, or pastel blues and pinks.

EASY-CARE GROUPING

Watering is the container gardener's main summer chore, but grouping your pots together in one area will make this task quicker and more convenient. Large, deep pots retain more water than shallow, small pots. Sunny patios get hot in summer, so use large pots in these areas (unless the plants withstand drought), placing smaller pots, which dry out quickly, in shady areas.

Try keeping small pots to the front of your display—not only is this more natural and pleasing visually, but it also makes it easier to sweep up any fallen flowers and leaves and generally to maintain and care for your plants.

Colorful pansies thrive in sun or part shade but will wilt immediately if the potting mix is dry—a handy sign that they need watering.

GROUPING FOR COLOR

Combine plants with bright colors to develop a kaleidoscopic effect or use contrasting colors such as blue and orange or yellow and purple for bold statements. Create more harmonious displays by mixing yellow with orange and red flowers; pink with white and red; or blue with mauve and purple.

TOP TIP IN THE WINTER MONTHS, MOVE POTS OF EVERGREEN SHRUBS FROM A SHADY AREA TO FORM A BACKDROP TO YOUR MAIN DISPLAY. THIS WILL ALSO FILL IN ANY GAPS LEFT BY TENDER PLANTS THAT HAD TO BE REMOVED DURING THE COLD PERIOD.

Use small pots of colorful flowers to lift and enliven your permanent display.

GROUPING FOR IMPACT

A solitary pot of flowers often looks lost, but can be striking alongside bigger foliage plants. So if a single plant is not as eye-catching as you had hoped, team it with smaller plants for added impact. Although they are pricey, try adding a large plant, which will transform a grouping if surrounded by smaller plants—clipped bay and olive trees are great investments and will last for years. Or bring height and balance to the back of your displays by placing small plants on upturned pots. You can also group different plants to emphasize each one's character, such as a strappy-leaved phormium with round-leaved hostas.

An eye-catching spiky phormium will bring contrasting shapes and colors to this arrangement all year.

DEVELOPING VERTICAL INTEREST

Height and presence are important to any garden planting, and especially so with container gardening. The containers themselves give even the smallest plant a boost above ground level, but a group of pots all planted to knee-height makes for a flat display. Be bold with statuesque plants, lift containers upward, and cover your walls: with container gardening, there are all sorts of ways to give your plantings a lift.

Japanese maples are among the most popular small trees for pots: slow-growing, with a graceful, filigree framework.

USING TALL PLANTS

Small tree species, such as Japanese maples (see above), are a great way to extend your planting upward. They can, however, be a long-term, slow-growing commitment. For more rapid results, consider adding height with annual climbers, which will allow you to vary your displays every year or so. Shrubs trained as standards provide height without bulk; choose evergreens such as boxwood and holly to maintain structure through the winter. Bamboos and grasses introduce strong vertical lines and are well-suited to modern, urban planting, while tall plants with lush, bold leaves can add the "canopy" element to a jungle theme.

Strong verticals and the "floating" flat flower heads of achilleas, held above their foliage, draw the eye upward.

RAISING POTS UP

A traditional stately urn on a plinth may be too grand for many small yards or terraces, but a whole range of other structures can be used to raise up your plant pots. An étagère (a tiered plant stand) can be stunning when used for themed collections of plants such as primulas, gazanias, or tulips. Ladders (purpose-built for plants or upcycled) are popular, but may not be sufficiently stable to support larger pots, especially if children or pets use the same space. Discarded pieces of furniture can be creatively recycled as stands for plant pots—old kitchen chairs, shelving units, and bedside tables are all good options. They will not last forever, but they will have enjoyed a useful second life.

A repurposed side table makes a great stand for container plants.

Soil-filled pockets provide homes for a mix of small flowering plants and kitchen herbs in this clever wall planter.

HANGING GARDENS

With the aid of hanging baskets and wall-mounted planters, you can easily furnish your outdoor space with interest at eye level, just as you would hang colorful artwork on the walls of a room. Because they are exposed to drying sun and wind, baskets are perhaps the most high-maintenance of containers, but results can be striking. Wire baskets will need to be lined before planting: cardboard and fiber liners can be bought, but a greener option is to use moss from your lawn.

On a sturdy trellis, you can use butcher's hooks to hang upcycled buckets, pierced with drainage holes— these are inexpensive and may be easier than baskets to keep moist in summer. You could also consider filling lengths of guttering with trailing plants. When attaching wall planters to vertical surfaces, always take account of the strength of the structure.

Hanging gardens need not be the traditional flower-stuffed baskets: more subtle and varied effects are possible.

VERTICAL PLANTING

The concept of plant walls first appeared in modern architecture as a way of "greening" city buildings. There are scaled-down domestic versions of these quite elaborate commercial systems, which rely on technology to keep the plants thriving, but they are expensive. There is, fortunately, a whole range of inexpensive, low-tech "plant-wall" planters on the market, consisting of planting pockets mounted on a backing sheet. Planters made from unobtrusive fabrics and recycled pallets are among the many options that will allow you to clad your outside walls with tapestries of color and texture.

CHOOSING YOUR POTS

You can grow plants in almost anything, from an ancient stone urn to a pair of old boots. Pots of similar size or material will always help unite your display, especially if you grow a wide range of plants; if your collection is more limited, a variety of containers will inject extra sparkle and interest. But the key to success is to prevent plant roots from sitting in water, so make sure that any excess water can drain away.

CHOOSING MATERIALS

Garden centers offer a wide range of pots in different sizes and materials. Terra-cotta is a great choice: its porosity helps prevent rot and disease and its earthy red color offsets most plants. Frost-resistant terra-cotta and glazed pots are usually undamaged in winter, but may crack if the potting mix freezes and expands. Wood insulates the roots all year and ages well; half barrels are a good choice and usually last many years.

Wicker baskets lined with plastic are attractive and lightweight but will only survive a few seasons. Thin materials such as plastic and metal are not as effective as concrete, stone, or terra-cotta in insulating roots from heat and cold, but they are lightweight.

In terms of environmental impact, local-made terra-cotta, although expensive, is by far the best choice. Many glazed pots are imported and plastic pots are not "green," but can be reused and will last for decades.

Pots in various sizes and materials highlight each container and suit a mix of similar plants.

Terra-cotta pots do not distract the eye from plants; they also drain well and are ideal for plants that dislike wet soil.

Unusual containers draw the eye and give otherwise plain plantings, such as these herbs, a fresh look.

SIZE OF POT

Large containers add drama, focus, and style to any garden display. Plants in large pots are also easier to care for. On the downside, they can be costly and heavy to move, especially when full. Most plants do not have roots that go deeper than 16 in (40 cm), so deep pots are essential only for trees. A group of small pots will be inexpensive and can be easily rearranged in your space, but elevate them from ground level to create more impact.

If you are buying a pot for a specific plant, choose one that is wider than the plant's current pot (see p.30). Leave room for the plant to grow, but make sure the pot is not so big it is swamped by empty, wet potting mix. If well fed and watered (see pp.24–27), most plants grow happily in pots that appear too small for them—a full pot packed with plants also looks more impressive.

These bowl-shaped pots contrast with the upright leaves of bearded iris and are deep enough for their roots.

SHAPE OF POT

Pots are available in a terrific range of shapes. Be wary of pots with curved sides or that are narrow at the top—if you plant perennials or shrubs directly into these it will be impossible to get them out when you need to move them to a larger pot. If you do want to plant a perennial into this style of pot, find a simple plastic one that sits neatly in the mouth of the container and plant into it. This will also mean you can change the plant display in the pot in just a few minutes.

Unlike perennials, annuals can be grown in any shape of container because they are disposed of at the end of every season. Use your imagination: upcycled old kitchen containers and watering cans—all kinds of items can be used, and can often enhance the shape of the plants they contain.

Plant perennials in a basic pot before placing in a curved or narrow-topped one.

POT FEET AND SAUCERS

Pot feet (supports that lift pots off the ground) aid drainage of potting mix and prevent worms from entering the pots. You can buy attractive pot feet to match your pots but you could also use bricks or pavers. Saucers are useful in summer to put under plants that need lots of water, but remove them in wet weather and winter to prevent waterlogging.

Lift pots off the ground to help avoid waterlogging and wet potting mix.

BUYING YOUR PLANTS

The plants you select for your containers will reflect your personal taste and style. If you want year-round color and fragrance, then short-term bedding plants, which can be changed at least twice a year, give terrific results. But if you prefer longer-lasting plants—perennials or shrubs and small trees should thrive for years—great choices include bold evergreens such as fatsias and olives or bay trees. Whatever your goals, to achieve success, you will need to consider your budget, where and when to buy your plants, and also, among other things, the best place in your yard or patio to put them.

GOOD PLANNING

There are a few simple points to think about before deciding which plants to buy for your container garden and where to buy them. For example, are the plants you may have set your heart on suitable for the intended site—will they thrive in sunny, shady, windy, or exposed areas? If you are planning a rooftop garden, think about the width of doorways and stairs and whether you will be able to move your pots and plants up there. It is also good to have a budget: if finances are tight, the cheapest and quickest way to fill your pots is with bedding plants: these give instant color, but you will need to change them every spring and fall.

Walls and fences protect plants and expand the range of plants you can buy.

GARDEN CENTERS AND OTHER OUTLETS

Browsing around garden centers is by far the most enjoyable way to select your plants. Here, they will help you choose plants that are best-suited to your area and give advice on growing. They will also stock large specimens, saving you several years of growing, but bear in mind that these are more costly. You can also buy from plant fairs, supermarkets, and markets—plants bought from these outlets are sometimes less expensive but may not always be in prime condition.

NEED TO KNOW
- Choose healthy plants with strong, new growth and lots of buds.
- Buy flowering plants that are dormant, not in full bloom, as they are less expensive.
- Avoid shrubs with roots growing out of the bottom of the pot.
- Do not buy plants swimming in water or that have dried-out leaves or a mass of dead flowers.
- Be cautious of herbaceous plants and shrubs that are sold in colorful prepacks in peat as they are often of poor quality.

Garden centers give great advice and are packed with plants all year.

Plug plants are inexpensive if sent by mail, but will need careful growing on.

BUYING BY MAIL

Many plant nurseries offer an online service, which is a good way to buy plants. These can be smaller than plants from garden centers and may only be sent when the plants are dormant, from October to March. But they are often less costly than in garden centers, and specialists offer a wider range. Pot your plants as soon as they arrive.

Online orders are great for small bedding plants and seedlings or plug plants, which must be grown on before planting in bigger pots. "Pot-ready" plants are also available and can be immediately put into their display pots.

WHEN TO PLANT?

Pot plants can be planted all year, but there are optimal times for most. Shrubs, for example, are best planted in winter and spring, but if well watered, any time is good. Bedding plants are usually planted twice yearly. Spring-flowering bedding (including wallflowers, daisies, violas, and pansies) are planted in fall and are winter-hardy; tulips and daffodils are planted at the same time. Plants for summer display, including summer bulbs such as lilies, are planted in spring. Most of these plants are not frost-tolerant, so do not plant them outside until May. In urban gardens and sheltered, coastal areas, you may be able to plant earlier. Small, plug plants are sensitive to cold and overwatering. If you buy plants early, protect them from frost on cold nights by covering with fleece.

Tulips need planting six months before they bloom but will amply reward your good planning with their colorful flowers.

PLANTING UP POTS

Most plants can be grown in pots, which means that there are lots of great options available to you, including trees, grasses, annuals, herbaceous plants, and alpines. You can plant your pots to build up a collection of favorites or to make lavish displays, combining plants of every type, even though some may have specific requirements. You can also choose to simply stick to one variety in a container or even to one large plant on its own—almost anything's possible.

Be adventurous in your planting, mixing a range of types if they will create the lavish display you are aiming for.

PLANTING SEPARATELY OR IN GROUPS

The main benefits of growing a single plant in a pot are that you can tailor the soil, feeding, watering, drainage, and general growing conditions precisely to that plant's specific requirements.

If mixing several plants in one pot, pick those of similar size, vigor, and cultural needs so that they all thrive. Bedding plants, discarded at the end of the season, are great for beginners eager to experiment with colors and combinations—mix them up together or add them among permanent plants as flashes of color. Avoid mixing hardy and tender plants in the same pot, as you will need to remove the tender ones at the end of summer. Also avoid crowding slow-growing plants with vigorous annuals in the same pot.

HOW TO PLANT UP SIMILAR PLANTS

By grouping plants with contrasting foliage but similar needs, such as ferns, you can create a thriving, eye-catching display. You can plant them at any time and they will flourish in shady areas.

1 Arrange broken pot pieces or gravel in the bottom of a container with drainage holes to prevent the holes from being blocked with potting mix.

2 Fill your pot to about 2 in (5 cm) from the top with commercial potting mix. Add controlled-release fertilizer to the mix.

3 Soak the roots of your plants well, then remove each from its pot.

Placing the tallest plants at the back, start adding plants to the container.

4 Fill any gaps between the roots of your plants with potting mix, then thoroughly water the display to settle the plants into place.

HOW CLOSE TO PLANT?

Overly cramped planting leaves plants without enough room to grow, and can cause fungal diseases. How many plants you put in a pot depends on what season you plant and how long you can wait for a "full" look. If planting small plug plants in spring, leave them room to grow. As plants become more mature, you can plant closer together, as they will have less and less growing left to do. By late summer, for example, you can combine plants so that they're almost touching, to create an instant effect. Fall-planted pots will not make significant growth through the cold months, so you can pack the plants in if you intend to replant in spring.

Planting small plug plants densely will allow the plants to intermingle with each other, creating a gentle, subtle effect.

PLANTING UP BULBS

Plant spring-flowering bulbs in fall. The approximate planting depth is 2½ times the height of the bulb below the surface. If planting for one season, the depth is not critical, but daffodils can be planted and will last for many years under perennials.

Planting bulbs in layers in containers (see *right*) is a great idea because it allows you to achieve maximum color and a longer display. Plant the largest bulbs first; then, after adding more potting mix, plant another layer between the tips of the lower bulbs. You can plant several layers of the same bulbs or different bulbs. For extra layers of summer color, plant gladioli, freesias, lilies, and tigridias in spring, before adding the usual bedding plants.

TOP TIP ARRANGE SHORTER, EARLY-FLOWERING BULBS AROUND THE EDGE OF THE POT SO THAT THE FOLIAGE OF LATER-FLOWERING, LARGER PLANTS WILL NOT HIDE THEIR BLOOMS.

Layer daffodils and irises with primroses to create a vibrant display.

1. In the first, or bottom layer, of your pot, put in larger plants, such as tulips and daffodils.

2. Add more potting mix and then, in your second layer, plant smaller bulbs.

NEED TO KNOW
- Use enriched potting mix for plants that will be in pots for over a year.
- When planting shrubs or trees, avoid putting small plants in huge pots; pot on into larger pots as the plants mature.
- Always soak the roots of your plants thoroughly before planting in order to keep them moist.
- Add watering-retaining gel crystals to your potting mix to help keep it moist.
- Put plants in pots at the same depth as they were in their original pots.

PLANTING UP WINDOW BOXES AND HANGING BASKETS

Hanging baskets and window boxes are easy ways to bring color to drab areas. Window boxes give double value: you can admire them from inside and outside and they can also provide terrific year-round color.

A well-filled hanging basket, with blooms tumbling over its sides, is also a spectacular sight, but be sure to select a sheltered spot, away from harsh winds; most plants are also happiest with a little shade.

A WINTER WINDOW BOX

Nothing is more effective in winter than a window box brimming with colorful plants. To achieve this, plant in fall so that plants establish before the cold sets in—plant close together for impact.

Small evergreen shrubs are ideal as the basis of winter displays: skimmias, for example, have bright red buds opening to fragrant flowers in spring. Choose golden choisya, conifers, heucheras, and bright sedge for contrast in leaf shape. In front of these, try trailing ivy, periwinkle, or violas for winter color. Push dwarf daffodils, tulips, or muscari in the box at planting time for extra color in spring.

1 Place expanded polystyrene or gravel at the bottom of your box for drainage, then add commercial potting mix so it almost fills the box.
2 Experiment with arranging your pots of plants on the surface before planting them. When you are happy with the look, water the plants, remove them from their pots, and then plant the largest first.
3 Continue to plant, carefully working potting mix in around the roots to avoid gaps, which cause roots to dry out. Finally, if you wish, pop in some spring-flowering bulbs (see p.19).
4 Water well, place the box on your windowsill, and secure if necessary.

Upright and trailing pelargoniums make a glorious summer display.

WINDOW BOXES IN SUN

Light, bright, sunny sills offer a wide range of planting options for summer window boxes. Herbs, such as lavender and thyme, and pelargoniums thrive in sunny places. Succulents such as sedums and sempervivums also work well in these sites—they are evergreen, so will last into fall and beyond in a box.

If you choose deep boxes to plant in it will increase the volume and weight of potting mix and make watering less of a chore in hot weather. Adding some extra organic matter also makes watering easier as it helps prevent shrinking when dry.

Wire baskets must be lined to retain potting mix. Moss is a popular choice.

BASKETS AND LINERS

Hanging baskets are widely available and come in various materials. Wire baskets are always a popular choice and can be lined with moss (see *above*) or with pre-formed coconut fiber (see *right*)—the latter is easy to use but does not always fit a basket perfectly. Wicker baskets with plastic liners are attractive and convenient—the plastic liner helps reduce the need to water. Solid plastic baskets last for many years and often have built-in saucers to reduce watering needs, but they are not as attractive as other options—until plants start cascading over the sides.

NEED TO KNOW

- Summer baskets need watering regularly—in midsummer, once or even twice a day is necessary.
- Once growing strongly, give your basket plants a high-potash feed to maintain growth and flowers.

PLANTING A SUMMER HANGING BASKET

Hanging baskets leap into action in summer, filling your patio with flowers and foliage at eye level (see *pp.64–75*). Plant up your summer baskets in spring. A 14 in- (35 cm-) diameter basket would need one central plant, four or five plants around it, and then, for a full look, four or five small trailing plants around the edge. If using tender plants, such as pelargoniums and begonias, keep the planted basket in a greenhouse until after the last spring frost; or plant later, after the danger of frost has passed.

If using plastic-lined baskets (see *below*), cut a few slits in the sides of the plastic for drainage. After planting up the basket, place it in a shady place for a week or so, if possible—this will allow the roots to establish before you hang the basket.

1 Stand your basket temporarily on a large pot to make planting easier. If using a pre-formed liner, trim it to fit your basket.
2 To help retain moisture, cut a circle from an old plastic bag to line the basket a third of the way up the sides.
3 Fill two-thirds of your basket with potting mix, then add time-release fertilizer and water-retaining gel and mix well.
4 Before planting, make sure the plants are well watered and the potting mix is moist. Plant the central, tallest plant first, in the middle of the basket, then the others around it. Finally, place any trailing plants around the edge. Add extra potting mix to fill in around them. Water thoroughly.

TOP TIP AS PLANTS GROW THEY NEED MORE WATER AND MORE FEEDING; IF BASKETS GET DRY, TAKE THEM DOWN AND SOAK THEM IN A BUCKET OF WATER.

PLANTING UP CLIMBERS

As well as being ideal for screening spaces, climbing plants are terrific for bringing scent and color to eye level in a garden or patio. Some climbers have sucker-like roots on the stems, some have tendrils, and others twine around or scramble over neighboring plants, but all need some form of support.

Growing in containers gives you the option to plant climbers up a wall or fence, on a frame such as an obelisk, or at the base of a trellis, affixed to a wall. Most climbers, apart from annuals, are likely to live longer than their supports, which will need maintenance, and also replacement after a few years.

Large, deep, heavy pots are often best for growing climbers up a support.

SELECTING CONTAINERS

Most climbers have vast root systems and are best in deep pots. These hold more potting mix and moisture and do not get as hot in summer as small pots. If planting to grow up a wall or trellis, a square pot or one with a flat back can be placed flush against the wall.

When planting up an obelisk, use low, wide pots that will remain stable when the support is covered with foliage. Heavy materials such as wood and stone are preferable to plastic, which may blow over.

PLANTING AGAINST WALLS AND TRELLISES

Climbers can transform your garden or patio by covering bare walls or fences in eye-catching blooms and foliage. Some plants, such as ivy, stick with aerial roots to walls or fences, while others will need a trellis, obelisk, or other framework to cling to, often with your help.

Many climbers flower only at the top of the plant and can be completely leafless at the base. You can remedy this by placing pots of plants in front of the climber to conceal any bare stems.

Depending on the size of the container and the vigor of the plant, you will need to repot the climber after a few years. This can be a tricky process when it is growing up a trellis, unless the plant can be pruned hard without any damage. So, when planting, avoid these issues by putting the climber into a larger pot than may seem ideal (see *left*).

At first, self-clinging climbers may need a bit of help to stick to a wall: tie existing stems horizontally to nails and wires in the wall or fence. As the new stems grow up the support they will naturally adhere to the surface, even if it is smooth, as in glass or plastic.

Clematis such as 'Étoile Violette' scramble up trellises, creating sheets of color for months. This cultivar flowers in late summer and is pruned hard in spring.

HOW TO PLANT UP AN IVY CONE

Add charm to your patio by growing ivy around a simple wire cone or other frame shape—you can buy these from your local garden center, which will have a range of styles. Adaptable, evergreen, and shade-loving ivy is the perfect plant to create this kind of quick topiary.

1 Fill a 10in (25 cm) container with enriched potting mix and plant three ivies around the edge. Untie them from the canes and gently lay the ends of the ivy over the side of the pot.

2 Ensure your cone fits on the surface of your pot, then place it into the potting mix, pushing the legs firmly in so that the cone is upright and central.

3 Wind the ivies evenly around the base of, and over, the frame. Take care to fill in around the base since plants rarely grow downward.

4 Thoroughly water in the plants. Keep pushing new growth through the wire to fill in the cone as it grows. As plants mature, they will need light trimming to keep the cone shape neat.

PLANTING AN OBELISK

Obelisks encourage sturdy growth, add height and a focal point to your garden, and allow your display to be seen from all sides. Using an obelisk in a container also means you can easily repot your plant into a bigger pot as it grows.

To get your climber to fill the obelisk and produce growth from base to tip, prune it hard after planting and wind new shoots round the outside. Clematis respond well to this treatment, which prevents a tangle of growth at the top. New shoots grow upward and can be trained to fill gaps. The support may need replacing by that time; or you can pop a larger support over the first and your plant will grow through it. Cover the bare base of the climber as it ages by planting annuals around the edge.

> **TOP TIP** STABILIZE YOUR DISPLAY BY RUNNING A WIRE FROM ONE SIDE OF THE BASE OF THE OBELISK, UNDER THE POT, AND UP THE OTHER SIDE.

An obelisk allows your climber to be displayed from all sides.

POTTING MIXES AND FERTILIZERS

The right potting mix is vital for the health of your container plants. The most popular are commercial mixes: these are clean to use, lightweight, readily available, and suit most plants. But some plants require special mixes, and shrubs and trees benefit from varieties enriched with time-release fertilizer.

Potting mixes contain only limited amounts of nutrients, so your plants will also benefit from feeding. There are two main options here: time-release, which will continue to feed your plants for many months; and liquid fertilizers, which act instantly but must be applied frequently throughout the summer.

CHOOSING POTTING MIX

Commercial mixes are based on partially decomposed organic matter and continue to decompose in the pots. They are better for annuals and biennials than for perennials and shrubs. Peat, a dwindling natural resource, is found in many varieties, so check before buying and avoid if possible. Instead, look out for peat-free mixes, many of which contain recycled materials. They vary in structure, which can affect watering and feeding requirements, so find an option that meets your needs and stick to it.

Potting mixes enriched with time-release fertilizer contain more nutrients and are easier to rewet if they dry out. Never use garden soil in pots: it contains worms that can block drainage holes, and sometimes also weeds, diseases, slugs, and other pests.

Use a lime-free mix for plants that demand acid soil, such as camellias and pieris. This is often called "cactus" or "palm" mix and it does not contain calcium. But calcium is a key nutrient for most plants, so you cannot use the mix for all your plants, unless you also apply a fertilizer high in calcium, like bone meal.

FEEDING YOUR PLANTS

Use liquid fertilizer weekly in the growing season to provide nutrients and water. Granular fertilizers such as pelleted chicken manure are useful in spring to boost shrub growth, but switch to liquid feeding after a month.

Time-release fertilizers are the ideal way to feed container plants. Each pellet is coated in a resin that releases the fertilizer only when it is warm and moist enough for growth. Most last four to six months and are best added to the potting mix at planting time.

Use potting mix (left) not garden soil (right) for plants: it is pest- and disease-free and will promote healthy growth.

Liquid fertilizers are diluted with water and give plants a fast-acting nutrient boost.

PLANT NUTRIENTS

Fertilizer is absorbed by plants only when it is combined with adequate water. Thus, liquid and soluble fertilizers are a popular way to feed plants. General fertilizers contain roughly equal amounts of the three major plant nutrients (nitrogen, phosphorus, and potassium), while specialized fertilizers contain more of one nutrient than the others in order to benefit specific plants or needs (see chart, below). Fertilizer manufacturers show the exact proportions of these nutrients on the pack of fertilizer.

The most popular liquid fertilizers are tomato fertilizers—proportionally high in potassium, they are suitable for all flowering plants. Liquid lawn fertilizers (without weed killer or moss killer) are high in nitrogen and ideal for feeding foliage plants such as fatsias and bamboo.

NUTRIENT	FOUND IN	PROMOTES
Nitrogen (N)	Lawn fertilizer	Lush shoot growth and foliage
Phosphorous (P)	Bone meal	Root growth
Potassium (K)	Tomato feed and rose feed	Flower and fruit production and hardening of shoots in fall

Make your own plant feed using nettle or comfrey leaves diluted with water.

ORGANIC FERTILIZERS

Organic fertilizers contain the same major nutrients as other types of fertilizers and have to break down in the potting mix to be released to the plants. They take longer to act than non-organic fertilizers, but they include many other nutrients that can boost plant growth. Another advantage is that they encourage beneficial soil bacteria and fungi that may not be present otherwise.

Some liquid fertilizers contain seaweed. While seaweed is not considered a fertilizer in its own right, as it lacks the main nutrients that are beneficial to plants (see chart, left), the trace elements it contains are helpful, and can be used in the form of a foliar feed, which is sprayed onto the leaves of (mainly sick) plants to boost growth.

Make your own organic nettle or comfrey tea to feed your plants by filling a bucket with fresh leaves and stems, covering with water and a lid, and leaving for a few weeks. The resulting liquor is a good supplementary feed, packed with trace elements. Dilute the mixture in a can to the color of weak tea and use it liberally on your plants.

Mix time-release fertilizer in potting mix before planting so your plants receive a steady supply of nutrients.

NEED TO KNOW

- Always follow fertilizer directions carefully and mix/dilute as advised.
- Never mix liquid fertilizers more strongly than recommended—it may damage the plant roots.
- Never pour liquid fertilizer onto dry potting mix—always water the plant first and then apply.
- There is no point applying fertilizer in winter when plants are not growing as it will simply be flushed away.

WATERING

Your container plants are very dependent on you for water: not only do they lack access to deeper levels of soil moisture, but also their foliage helps keep rain off the surface of the potting mix in the pot, like a leafy umbrella. Regular watering will ensure that they are at their best. Choosing large pots can pay dividends here: the greater the volume of mix in the container, the better able it will be to retain moisture.

Hanging baskets are particularly vulnerable to drying out; a wand extension for your hose makes watering easy.

OPTIMAL WATERING

The answer to the question "when should I water a plant?" is emphatically not "when it looks like it needs a drink." Every time a plant wilts and then has to be revived, its strength is depleted and it will spend most of its time recovering, rather than performing well. You need to ensure that the plant has a steady supply of water to its roots. Testing the weight of containers will, in time, give you a good idea of whether they need water; if the pot is too big, stick your finger into the potting mix. Surprisingly, we cannot actually feel the sensation of wetness—but if the mix feels cool and spongy, it is moist, and if it feels warm and scratchy, it is dry. If you know you are not the most assiduous plant carer, choose plants that are suited to hot, dry sites (see pp.128–139); many have their own built-in "reservoirs," such as fleshy stems or leaves, or other adaptations that make them better able to stand neglect. Equally important is not to overwater: potting mix that remains sodden with stagnant water will, literally, drown your plants as their roots need air to function. Ensure your containers have good drainage at the base; in wet winters, take pots out of saucers and, if possible, stand them instead on pot feet.

Lots of plants competing for resources need lots of water; line open-sided containers such as this wicker box to hold moisture in.

Overwatering plants is as damaging as underwatering them. Use pot stands or tiles to elevate your pots and help drainage.

EFFECTIVE WATERING

Water the potting mix, not the plant's leaves and flowers, or most will run off and be wasted. On a really hot day, droplets of water on foliage can also scorch leaves as it evaporates. Watering straight from the watering-can spout or hose end will tend to create "craters" in the potting mix; either use a rosette or spray, or water onto something that will break up the flow, such as a crock or piece of tile placed in the pot. Water each pot thoroughly, rather than splashing from plant to plant.

Reviving a plant that has completely dried out is especially difficult when it is in a container. If the potting mix has dried out it will shrink, and water will run straight down the sides of the pot and out at the bottom. To remedy this, stand the plant in a bowl of water so that it can rewet from the base; if it is difficult to do this, gently water and water again until it is clear that the water is being absorbed into the potting mix.

A gentle flow of water using a rosette will prevent potting mix from being washed away, exposing fine feeder roots.

Collect runoff in a crate or bowl when watering baskets, and use it on other plants.

REUSE, RECYCLE

Most "gray water" from the house is absolutely fine for plants, especially if you alternate it with tap or rain water. Do not use anything containing harsh detergents; avoid using dish washing water that contains grease and cooked food particles, or you risk bad smells. Water used for scrubbing vegetables, rinsing rice, or soaking beans is perfect.

Rainwater is an increasingly valuable resource, and in hard-water areas, lime-hating plants such as camellias will particularly enjoy it. Not everyone has room for a rain barrel—even so, it is worth putting out your watering cans when a downpour is forecast.

WATERING AIDS

For large pots containing large plants, a plastic bottle with the base cut off, sunk upside down into the potting mix when planting, is a boon, enabling you to send water straight down to the roots (you can disguise it with underplanting). A "wand" attachment for your hose makes light work of watering hanging baskets. There are commercial reservoir systems for sinking into pots, with a wick that ensures a slow, as-needed supply; these can be invaluable while you are on vacation.

Customizable pot irrigation kits are also widely available, and make watering virtually effortless. Comprising narrow watering "spurs" leading from a hose that you can tuck behind your pots, they water all your plants at the turn of a tap; you can even install a timing device between the tap and the hose so that your plants almost water themselves.

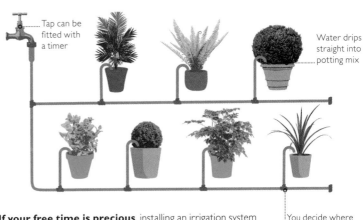

Tap can be fitted with a timer

Water drips straight into potting mix

You decide where to locate the spurs

If your free time is precious, installing an irrigation system will allow you to sit back and enjoy your garden after work, rather than tending to your plants; it is also water-efficient.

TOP TIP IRRIGATION KITS ARE EASIER TO ASSEMBLE IF YOU LAY ALL THE TUBING OUT IN THE SUN FOR A COUPLE OF HOURS FIRST. THE WARMTH SOFTENS THE PIPING, MAKING IT EASIER TO INSERT THE SPURS AND GUIDE THE HOSE AROUND YOUR POTS.

GROOMING AND SPRING CLEANING

Whatever you choose to plant in your containers, a little care and attention can transform ordinary displays into showstoppers. Incorporating grooming tasks into your usual routines will not only bring you greater pleasure from your garden, it will also make your plants stronger and healthier. Removing old flowers and leaves also often unveils problems such as pests, and whether your plants need extra feeding.

Keeping the area around your pots clean and tidy not only looks good but also discourages pests and diseases.

DEADHEADING FLOWERS

Plants produce flowers in order to make seeds, but once they have produced the seed pods, many of them simply do not bother to make any more blooms. Removing old flowers, or deadheading, encourages more blooms to grow, so it is a task that makes your plants thrive, look good, and stay colorful longer. It also prevents debris from falling from the plants and causing paving stones to become slippery and unsightly.

Pinch off large blooms, such as petunias and violas, making sure that you remove the whole bloom, with the seed pod, not just the petals. Plants with small flowers, such as diascias and nemesias, should have their flower clusters trimmed off as soon as the last flowers have dropped.

Roses require slightly different deadheading treatment from other plants. Remove old flowers by cutting them off along with a length of stem back to the highest large leaf to promote fast rebloom and keep plants compact.

TOP TIP SOME PLANTS THAT ARE GROWN SPECIFICALLY FOR THEIR FOLIAGE, SUCH AS COLEUS, BENEFIT FROM HAVING THEIR FLOWERS PINCHED OFF AS SOON AS THEY APPEAR, TO PROMOTE MORE, AND FLASHIER, FOLIAGE.

Coleus produce better foliage if you remove flowers as soon as they appear.

NEED TO KNOW

- Pull up weeds as soon as they appear and before they spread seeds onto other pots.
- Remove badly diseased plants from your groups of pots.
- Trim back deciduous plants in the fall to remove hiding places for pests.
- Check the rims of pots in dry weather for sheltering snails.

Pinching off faded flowers, along with their seed pods, keeps plants tidy and also encourages more flowers to bloom.

FROST DAMAGE IN SPRING

Many popular patio plants are slightly tender and likely to suffer from frost damage in winter. Snip off frosted shoots of plants such as choisya and give lavenders and sage a light prune in mid-spring. Other plants, including pieris and Japanese maples, tend to respond to the first hints of spring warmth by pushing out soft growth that can get caught by a late frost. Prune back these and new growth will appear. Prevent damage by covering plants with fleece at night when frost is forecast.

Cold damages the leaves of many evergreens during the winter months.

CLEANING POTS

Green algae on terra-cotta, stone, and concrete pots will not harm your plants, and can soften their appearance, but it may not be the look you are aiming for. If this is the case, pots can be easily scrubbed with patio cleaner and water.

If moss is allowed to build up around the base of pots, it can impede the drainage of the potting mix, so it is a good idea to sometimes move and clean the area around the pots. Also check your pots for cracks and sweep up any debris that could provide shelter for woodlice, snails, and slugs, which may attack young plants.

Aged and weathered pots may be in keeping with your garden style and add rustic charm to your displays.

PRUNING

Many shrubs require light pruning: to do this, pinch out the growing tips of young plants in spring to encourage a bushier habit and a fuller appearance. Regular, light pruning is often better than allowing a plant to get too big and then pruning hard, which will reduce flowering.

Some plants profit from pruning in order to shape and enhance their overall look. Bamboos, for example, benefit from removal of the lower branches to show off their stems and some shoots; likewise, Japanese maples and pieris, to reveal their stems and allow underplanting with spring bulbs.

Prune back shoots before midsummer to prompt new growth and bushier plants.

Pinch out young tips in springtime to encourage plants to branch out.

REPOTTING AND TOP-DRESSING

Some of your container plants will be chosen for seasonal color and then discarded. Others will become your pride and joy, growing bigger and more beautiful each year—and as they mature they will need to be moved into larger pots. These new containers will accommodate their roots and provide a bigger reservoir of water, but they will also keep them stable and less likely to blow over as they get taller.

Mature plants are difficult to repot, so it is often easier to keep them healthy by top-dressing them with fresh potting mix.

REPOTTING YOUR PLANTS

Established plants will not need repotting every year, but while small enough to be able to lift and manage they will benefit from repotting every few seasons. It is important to replant into pots that are only slightly larger than the original pot—about 3–4 in (8–10 cm) wider and a little deeper. If small plants are transferred into large pots and surrounded by wet potting mix they may be overwhelmed and struggle to grow. When potting shrubs, use an enriched potting mix because the plant will remain in it for several years.

HOW TO REPOT

1 Choose a pot with drainage holes that is slightly larger than the pot you are repotting from. Fill the new pot with potting mix to approximately the same level it was in the old pot.

2 Water the plant and remove it from its old pot. If repotting when the plant is dormant, gently tease out the roots if they seem compacted.

3 Put the plant in place, checking the level is correct. Add more potting mix around the edges, filling any gaps.

4 Water to settle the plant and fill in any large air pockets.

ROOT TRIMMING

If you cannot find a suitable larger pot to repot your plant into, you can keep it healthy by replacing the lower level of potting mix in winter or spring. To do this, gently lay the plant on its side, pull it from the pot, and chop off the lower quarter or third of the soil, along with the roots. Turn the pot upright again, put in the same amount of fresh potting mix, and replace the plant. Give it a thorough soak to help the plant recover.

With the plant on its side, pull it from the pot—you may need help with this.

Cut away the soil from the base of the root ball before repotting.

TOP-DRESSING

When a tree or shrub becomes too large to repot, it can be maintained for several years by top-dressing. This straightforward task is best done in the early spring and involves scraping off some of the old potting mix from the surface of the pot and discarding it.

Replace the old potting mix with fresh mix combined with time-release fertilizer to feed the plant through the entire growing season. This helps avoid compaction of the soil surface and also removes weeds. If the surface is covered in gravel, simply remove this first and then replace it after top-dressing.

Replace old potting mix from the top of the pot with new mix.

Add time-release fertilizer to feed your plants throughout the season.

NEED TO KNOW
- Commercial potting mix must be changed every two years: its organic content decomposes, causing the mix to shrink and roots to dry out in summer and drown in winter.
- Most perennials will benefit from an enriched potting mix with coarse sand and time-release fertilizer.
- In the second season, enrich your commercial potting mix with fertilizer or, alternatively, replace the top half of the pot with fresh mix.
- If you are growing shrubs on rooftop gardens or balconies, use an enriched potting mix without sand—this will reduce the weight of the pot.

WHAT TO DO WITH OLD POTTING MIX

Old potting mix from pots that have grown flowers (see *Need to Know, left*) can be spread on the surface of the garden as a mulch or dug in: it may not contain many nutrients, but it will help improve your garden soil. If there is any chance that your old mix may contain pests such as vine weevil grubs (see p.36), spread it on a plastic sheet on the driveway or lawn before adding it to your garden so that birds have a chance to feast on the pests.

Old potting mix can be used as mulch or dug in to improve your soil.

TOP TIP BULBS CAN BE PLANTED IN THE SAME POT AS SHRUBS. CHOOSE DAFFODILS THAT CAN BE PLANTED 3 IN (8 CM) BELOW THE SURFACE SO THAT THEY ARE NOT DISTURBED WHEN TOP-DRESSING.

OVERWINTERING

Many perennial container plants are hardy and will not need special attention in winter. Others will want a bit of extra care to survive until the next season, including protection from cold and excess moisture in the potting mix. Containers may need safeguarding from frost. Winter is also the time to tidy up fallen leaves, clean the paving and pots, and prepare for the tremendous excitement of spring.

Provide temporary protection from frost by covering your plant with fleece during the cold winter months.

BRINGING PLANTS UNDER COVER

Some temporary summer plants need protection from frost. Every space has microclimates, and patios (especially if they are sunny) are often far less cold than other areas of your yard and may escape frost, except in very cold winters. Even so, plants such as bananas, heliotropes, and begonias will need to be kept under cover. Begonias, dahlias, and cannas will die down to tubers and corms. After this has happened, store them somewhere dry, cool, and frost-free for the winter.

Fuchsias and other plants that lose their leaves during the winter months can be kept somewhere cool with little light, but be sure to check that they are barely moist. Evergreens do best if they are kept in a bright but cool spot — a polytunnel or greenhouse is ideal. If available, a conservatory or sunny windowsill in a cool room in the home is perfect for small plants and succulents.

Move succulents to a windowsill or conservatory during the winter.

PROTECTING ROOTS

Plants in containers are more vulnerable to frost than the same plants growing in the ground because frost can access roots from all sides, not just from the top. To stop potting mix freezing, move pots near the house, where heat from the walls will protect them, but keep them watered. Alternatively, wrap the pots with bubble wrap, but do not cover the surface or the plants as this can cause rot; use fleece to cover the plants themselves. You can also fill black trash bags with newspaper and tie these around the pots. A more efficient method is to line the inside of the pot with bubble wrap before planting, which helps prevent the pots cracking when the potting mix freezes.

Lining your pots with bubble wrap will protect both the pots and the plant roots.

Wood is a good insulator and will help protect the plant's roots from the cold.

PROTECTING EVERGREENS

Evergreens are not completely dormant in winter, so be sure to water them during these months. The plants do not wilt if temporarily dry and the symptoms will only appear months later, when the leaves turn brown. Containers should be wrapped to stop the potting mix from freezing, which will prevent the roots absorbing water. Cover the foliage with fleece, secured by pegs and string, to protect the plants from cold and drying winds—fleece bags of different sizes are widely available. Fleece should be loosely applied and only used for a few weeks: if left longer than this, it can prompt premature growth in spring and make the plant vulnerable to late frosts. To prevent the potting mix waterlogging and damaging the roots, make sure your evergreens are removed from any saucers they were in during the summer.

TOP TIP MOVE TALL AND TOP-HEAVY PLANTS TO SHELTERED SPOTS TO PREVENT GALES FROM KNOCKING THEM OVER AND DAMAGING BOTH THE PLANTS AND THE POTS.

Terra-cotta pots can crack and split if they become wet and frozen in winter.

PROTECTING POTS

Damaged containers during winter can prove costly if they need to be replaced. To avoid this, do not leave empty pots of potting mix outside—the mix will freeze, expand, and then split both terra-cotta and ceramic. Filled pots are also a perfect place for snails and slugs to lay eggs; snails also like to overwinter under the lips of pots.

Terra-cotta is absorbent and, if wet, the surface can split and chip when it freezes, so move empty pots into a shed in winter or store them upside down under a plastic sheet. Keep wooden troughs empty and dry, too: this will also allow you to make any essential repairs to them and apply preservative.

PROBLEM SOLVING

If you water and feed your plants they should grow, flower, and be healthy. Sometimes, however, things can go wrong, even if you love and nurture your plants. For example, weather is notoriously fickle and different parts of your garden will have different microclimates, affecting the way your plants grow. Fortunately, most plant problems can be solved or prevented by following some quite simple steps.

If plants are badly under-watered or subject to strong, drying winds, their leaf tips will turn brown.

Pelargoniums can suffer fungal diseases if dead flowers fall onto its lower leaves.

If you forget to water your bamboo for long periods, the leaves will turn brown.

Begonias, like many plants, are sensitive to frost, which turns growth to mush.

Yellow older leaves in summer could be nitrogen deficient, so feed plants more.

LEAF PROBLEMS

Problems with leaves are often clear indicators that a plant is ailing. Keeping a look out for changes in leaf color will help you identify any problems and remedy them as soon as possible.

CRISP BROWN LEAF TIPS and edges, frequently in Japanese maples, are caused by lack of water and cold, drying wind. Drought can also lead to older leaves, often in the center of a plant, turning yellow, then brown, and then dropping off completely. Leaves are also damaged by water splashed on them in hot sun, the drops acting like lenses, burning the foliage. Avoid watering in hot sun to prevent this. Late spring frost can result in new, soft growth blackening and withering.

YELLOW BLOTCHES OR STRIPES on leaves are often caused by viral diseases. Lilies, dahlias, and cannas frequently suffer from viruses, which are commonly spread by aphids (see p.36) and cannot be cured, so plants have to be destroyed.

YELLOW LEAVES may mean your plant requires more feeding. Acid-loving plants develop yellow foliage with green veins if planted in limey potting mix: watering with chelated iron and an acid plant food can correct this.

FLOWER PROBLEMS

A plant's inability to flower and retain flowers is due to many issues—most of which are easily dealt with.

LACK OF FLOWERS can result from too much shade. Pruning affects flowering, too: so always prune at the specified time. Some plants hate root disturbance and dividing them can lead to poor flowering. Too much feeding, especially with high-nitrogen fertilizers, promotes leaf growth at the expense of flowers.

PREMATURE FLOWER AND BUD DROP and wilting are frequently caused by drought. Heavy infestations of aphids will also kill developing flowers.

Dead flower buds on lilies and daffodils can be caused by the plant drying out.

Poor drainage leads to waterlogging and roots dying. The plant may turn yellow, drop leaves, or die as a result.

POOR GROWTH

Lack of healthy growth is usually related to watering and feeding. If plants dry out too much between watering they will struggle and never make good growth. If they are not fed enough, their growth will be stunted with small, pale leaves, often flushed with red or purple.

Poor potting mix structure—a common problem with all mixes after several years in the pot—leads to root problems through drying out in summer and waterlogging in winter. If plants are kept in the same potting mix and container for many years, they become pot-bound, filling the pot with roots and depleting the nutrients.

WHY DID IT DIE?

Plants can die for many reasons. First, always check your plant is not an annual, which will die in late summer anyway. Otherwise, plants wilt in summer if dry, and will need immediate watering. But waterlogged plants also wilt, because the roots are unable to supply sufficient moisture to the stems and leaves. These can rarely be saved.

Plants often survive winter but then fail to grow in spring because the roots were damaged by winter cold and wet.

Underfeeding can cause poor growth, unusually small leaves, and poor leaf color.

Boxwood frequently becomes bronzed when dry and starved, but will recover.

NEED TO KNOW

- Some plants are prone to disease: for example, roses suffer from rust, blackspot (see p.61), and mildew (see p.37); verbenas and clematis are also affected by mildew.
- Modern cultivars are often bred with resistance to diseases and these help make growing in containers more successful.
- Compact cultivars need less pruning and are easier to care for in exposed situations.

PESTS AND DISEASES

Container plants are affected by the same pests and diseases as plants elsewhere in the garden. Some, like slugs, are less likely to be a real nuisance, while others, especially vine weevils, are more problematic in pots. Choose disease-resistant plants, and check them often—the sooner you spot problems, the more easily you can control them.

ANTS

PROBLEM Ants carry aphids and scale insects over plants, disturbing soil and roots, and killing plants in the process.
CAUSE Nesting ants in potting mix.
REMEDY Ants prefer dry conditions, so more regular watering may dissuade them. Use bait stations and ant-control powders on the patio. A pathogenic nematode may reduce activity.

VINE WEEVILS

PROBLEM Irregular notches develop on the edges of evergreen leaves, including viburnums and euonymus. Plants wilt because the roots are eaten by grubs. Sempervivums, begonias, fuchsias, and heucheras are commonly affected.
CAUSE Dark gray adults eat leaves and lay tiny eggs in soil in summer. These hatch into grubs that eat the roots of plants until they pupate, to emerge as adults in spring or late summer.

REMEDY Clear debris in and around pots to prevent adults hiding there. Damage to evergreens indicates that grubs are present, eating roots. Cover soil surface with grit to dissuade egg laying. If plants collapse, tip out potting mix and pick out grubs. Control larvae in the potting mix with parasitic nematodes, "watered" onto it in late spring and summer. This is most effective if the potting mix is not allowed to dry out.

APHIDS

PROBLEM Green, brown, or black sap-sucking insects cause stunting, distortion of growth, and spread of viral diseases. Widespread on a range of plants.
CAUSE Aphids cluster on young shoots. Stressed, dry plants are most affected.
REMEDY Ladybugs and hoverflies are predators. Rub off aphid clusters by hand. Most insecticides control them.

ADULT VINE WEEVIL

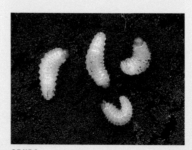

GRUBS

CATERPILLARS

PROBLEM Irregular patches of leaves are eaten, often with main veins remaining.
CAUSE A wide range of caterpillars eat various plants, before turning into moths or butterflies.
REMEDY Pick off caterpillars at night: they often hide by day. Synthetic and organic sprays are effective against most, but also harm beneficial insects.

LILY BEETLES

PROBLEM Patches of lily leaves and buds are eaten. Black, slimy lumps are left on stems and leaves.
CAUSE The bright red lily beetle eats the plants and lays eggs; the black substance is the grubs' excrement.
REMEDY Pick off adults and grubs when seen. Spray with systemic insecticide only when plants are not in bloom.

SCALE INSECTS

PROBLEM Leaves become sticky. White, fluffy areas develop on branches and trunks in summer. Brown lumps also appear on stems and under leaves.
CAUSE Sap-sucking insects that do not move from feeding site. Poorly fed and watered plants are most affected.
REMEDY If on small areas, pick off; otherwise, use systemic insecticide.

SLUGS AND SNAILS

PROBLEM Areas of leaves and flowers disappear, often just stalks remain.
CAUSE Slugs (if damage is close to the ground) or snails (if it is higher up).
REMEDY Clear debris. Look under and around pots during the day. Cover potting mix with grit or eggshells. Put copper strips or petroleum jelly around pot rims. Use beer traps and slug baits.

POWDERY MILDEW

PROBLEM White, powdery coating appears on leaves; it can turn black and distorted. Roses, begonias, verbenas, and clematis are often affected.
CAUSE A fungal growth.
REMEDY Poor nutrition and dryness at the roots encourage mildew. Keep potting mix moist. Spray with a fungicide to prevent mildew.

SOOTY MOLD

PROBLEM Black, sticky coating on leaves of evergreens—including camellias and bay trees—that weakens the plant.
CAUSE Sticky honeydew excreted by the scale insect is colonized by sooty mold fungus, which stops light reaching leaves.
REMEDY Wash off the fungus with water and soft soap. Control the scale insects to stop further problems (see *above*).

Include a few plants for their height or dramatic shapes to lift your display from the ordinary to the spectacular. Cordylines and yuccas are deservedly popular for their spiky outlines.

FOR HEIGHT AND STRUCTURE

Patio displays sometimes lack height and structure, but a few simple ideas can help bring both elements into play. Investing in a couple of tall, standout plants, for example, can often introduce, balance, drama, and vertical interest.

LEADING THE EYE UPWARD

Plants that grow straight up will contrast with those that are more bushy to help bring height, balance, and structure to your patio. Bamboos are great in this respect, combining narrow, vertical stems, often in intriguing colors, and delicate leaves that move in the slightest breeze and always look elegant. Another tall grass, *Miscanthus sinensis*, dies down each year and has to be trimmed in spring, but is also good for vertical interest, especially in fall, when many plants produce fluffy heads of flowers. Slender, upright conifers look good all year and work particularly well in formal plantings; they are ideal for framing views and contrasting with looser-growing plants.

STRUCTURAL CONTRASTS

If you are eager to add structural impact to your display, then standards, with contrasting straight stems and ball-shaped heads, are popular and always effective. This is how most people grow bay trees (*Laurus nobilis*), with stems ranging

3 ft 3 in–6 ft 6 in (1–2 m)—they are guaranteed to bring a strong focus at any time of year. Olives are grown the same way but create a lighter look, with more diffuse, gray leaves, and are ideal in a hot, sunny spot. Equally popular as standards are flamingo willows. Although not evergreen, their pink-flushed leaves are eye-catching in summer and easy to grow.

LEAVES OF ALL SHAPES

When you need something dramatic to bring structure and texture to a grouping, large foliage always fits the bill. For light shade, *Fatsia japonica* is the perfect choice—its large, shiny, fingered leaves are always striking, and as plants get taller and are seen from below rather than above, they are increasingly beautiful. Large windmill palms are the most imposing plant you can include in your displays, but take several decades to reach the size when they will tower over you; but they are stunning even when small. The same is true of cordylines—with their clusters of long, narrow leaves—which are magnificent both as small plants and as towering trees.

CANNA LILY _CANNA_

These are tall, bold plants with dramatic looks and, with winter protection, they will grow again next year. Canna lilies may not always flower, but their big, paddle-shaped leaves, in a multitude of colors, are striking— their bright, showy blooms are an extra bonus.

PLANT TYPE Half-hardy perennial; needs protection below 45°F (7°C)

HEIGHT Up to 3 ft 3 in–6 ft 6 in (1 m–2 m) in a pot

SPREAD Up to 3 ft 3 in (1 m) in a pot

POT SIZE One plant per 12 in- (30 cm-) diameter pot; three plants per 24 in- (60 cm) diameter pot

☼ ☼

CALENDAR

	WINTER	SPRING	SUMMER	FALL
IN LEAF				
IN FLOWER				

COLOR

LEAVES Chocolate-brown to mid-green, often striped with orange, pink, or acid-yellow

FLOWERS Pink, crimson, scarlet, orange, apricot, yellow

Divide canna lilies in spring, and start sections in warmth for early flowers.

CHOOSE

Canna lilies come in a range of sizes, so it is always a good idea to check varieties before buying them to make sure you get the height you need for your garden or patio. The plants grow from rhizomes that are sold in early spring—try to find plump ones with plenty of "eyes." To save yourself time and effort, you can buy growing plants in garden centers throughout the spring and summer.

Canna indica TROPICANNA GOLD is a great choice, with orange flowers. _C. × generalis_ Cannova Series are compact, flower freely, and are also a good choice.

PERFECT PARTNERS Make canna lilies the stars of hot, bright combinations, or pair them with bold-leaved, jungle plants. **LARGE** _Cordyline australis, Fatsia japonica, Trachycarpus fortunei_ **MEDIUM** _Agapanthus, Dahlia, Euphorbia characias_ **SMALL** _Heuchera, Hosta, Yucca_

PLANT

Dry canna-lily rhizomes should be started into growth from spring to summer in small pots in a warm place indoors. They can be planted outside, if they are growing strongly, when all danger of frost has passed. These greedy plants need potting mix with added time-release fertilizer. Plant them in the center of a large pot surrounded by smaller plants.

GROW

Water your plants regularly and give them a boost with an extra liquid feed after midsummer. As flowers in the flower head fade, snap them off with your fingers and thumb to keep the plants looking good. When a whole flower head has no new blooms, cut back the entire stem, leaves, and all. New, leafy stems will grow, even if there is not time for them to flower.

MAINTAIN When their season is over, you can overwinter cannas under cover, watering sparingly. The stems will die down but the rhizomes will survive. If you do not have shelter, try wrapping the pot; in mild areas and cities, there is a good chance plants will come through the winter. When older plants outgrow their containers, you can split them up in spring and repot the best sections.

TROPICANNA GOLD has magnificent striped leaves and burnt-orange flowers.

CABBAGE PALM

CORDYLINE AUSTRALIS

Young cabbage palms form a rosette of grasslike leaves at ground level, up to 3 ft 3 in (1 m) tall. After a few years, as new leaves grow at the top and old ones fall at the base, they develop a palmlike trunk. Any problems with these plants are generally caused by cold winds and winter wet.

PLANT TYPE Evergreen shrub; frost hardy to frost tender; needs protection from cold winds and winter wet

HEIGHT Up to 9 ft 9 in (3 m) in a pot

SPREAD Up to 4 ft 9 in (1.5 m) in a pot

POT SIZE One plant per 12 in- (30 cm-) diameter pot

☼ ☼

CALENDAR

	WINTER	SPRING	SUMMER	FALL
IN LEAF				
IN FLOWER				

COLOR

LEAVES Deep burgundy, bronze, green striped with coral, yellow or cream, or silvery pink

FLOWERS Creamy white

Bundle and wrap the leaves loosely if exceptionally cold weather is forecast.

'Torbay Red' is quite hardy and ideal in cool-temperate climates.

CHOOSE

Cabbage palms are easy-care plants, but they vary in their tolerance of cold weather, so choose the hardiest if you live in a cold area. 'Torbay Red' has bronze-red leaves and is more reliable in cold gardens. However, the variegated 'Torbay Dazzler' will struggle in exposed areas. The green- and red-leaved cordylines are often grown from seed, so they are far less costly than variegated kinds.

PERFECT PARTNERS Combine the spiky form with other textural plants, and underplant with bright flowers. **LARGE** *Fatsia japonica, Laurus nobilis, Musa basjoo* **MEDIUM** *Aeonium arboreum, Phormium, Pseudopanax lessonii* **SMALL** *Astelia chathamica, Osteospermum, Penstemon*

PLANT

If you buy and plant cabbage palms in spring, they will be well established by fall and more likely to survive the winter. Green-leaved varieties will tolerate light shade, but those with colored leaves should be positioned in full sun or their vivid hues may fade.

Cabbage palms must have good drainage, so use potting mix labeled for palms and put plenty of broken pot pieces in the bottom of the container.

GROW

Water plants freely in summer but sparingly in winter. Feed weekly with a balanced, liquid fertilizer from spring to late summer. Top-dress or repot if necessary in spring. Mature plants may surprise you by sending up a flowering stem in summer. Pull off or cut faded or damaged leaves back to their base.

MAINTAIN In winter, move pots to a sheltered site, perhaps beside the house. When rain accumulates in the growing point, at the base of the young leaves, plants can rot. Prevent this either by bringing them under cover, or by bundling and wrapping up their leaves during very frosty weather.

FALSE CASTOR OIL PLANT *FATSIA JAPONICA*

This bold, large-leaved evergreen makes a big statement, its hand-shaped, glossy leaves contrasting with smaller foliage plants. Whether a young plant or a mature specimen, it creates a tropical look and is often a prized possession.

PLANT TYPE Hardy, evergreen shrub; needs protection below 23°F (–5°C)

HEIGHT 6 ft 6 in (2 m) in a pot, more when mature

SPREAD 6 ft 6 in (2 m) in a pot

POT SIZE One plant per 12 in- (30 cm-) diameter pot; needs a larger pot when mature. Note that the large, older plants may lean heavily due to the weight of their leaves and may require support

CALENDAR

	WINTER	SPRING	SUMMER	FALL
IN LEAF				
IN FLOWER				

COLOR

LEAVES Rich green in part shade; may be yellow-green in sunnier positions

FLOWERS White

CHOOSE

You will find this plant in the "outside shrubs" or "houseplants" sections of garden centers. If sold as a houseplant, it will have soft, tender foliage, so only move it outside during the summer. Variegated kinds, including 'Spider's Web' (with green leaves shaded in white), will brighten any shady patio.

Offset young fatsias with trailing foliage from temporary summer plants.

PERFECT PARTNERS The magnificent leaves are always imposing, but particularly stunning in a jungle planting of foliage plants. **LARGE** *Laurus nobilis, Musa basjoo, Pseudopanax* **MEDIUM** *Euonymus, Phormium, Viburnum* **SMALL** *Buxus sempervirens, Liriope spicata, Vinca major*

PLANT

False castor oil plants can be planted all year, but spring to fall is best. Small plants may have clusters of seedlings: prune off all but three of these, at the base, so that each can grow without being crowded. Large, mature plants cast deep shade on the pot surface, so do not underplant them. Use enriched potting mix to keep the plant nourished.

GROW

Keep the plant moist at all times, especially in winter. The large leaves direct rain away from the pot surface so it can dry out, even in wet weather. Although tough, it will grow more rapidly if well fed: feed weekly in the growing period, but stop in September to prevent late flushes of new foliage that can be damaged by early frosts.

MAINTAIN If your plants grow taller than you like, simply prune off the tops in spring and they will sprout to create a fuller, bushier plant.

Large clusters of tiny, white, late-fall flowers develop into black berries. In late winter or spring, prune these off to tidy the plant and remove yellow and browning leaves.

Prune shoots in spring to maintain large plants at a manageable size.

UPRIGHT JUNIPER

JUNIPERUS SCOPULORUM 'SKYROCKET'

Slim and distinctive, an upright conifer adds punctuation to every grouping. It will contrast with and also draw the eye to almost every other nearby plant, especially those that are planted around its base. The conifer's fine, evergreen foliage is a welcome sight all year.

PLANT TYPE Hardy, evergreen shrub
HEIGHT Up to 8ft 2in (2.5m) in a pot
SPREAD Up to 12in (30cm) in a pot
POT SIZE One plant per 12in- (30cm-) diameter pot; needs repotting after two years
☼

CALENDAR

	WINTER			SPRING			SUMMER			FALL		
IN LEAF	■	■	■	■	■	■	■	■	■	■	■	■
IN FLOWER												

COLOR

LEAVES Blue-green
FLOWERS Insignificant

CHOOSE

This narrow, upright conifer will draw attention in any display. The handsome shrub is usually sold when it is about 24in (60cm) high. It grows quickly, so there is no need to buy a larger, more expensive plant, unless you want an immediate effect.

Alternatives, also with a bold form, include *Cupressus sempervirens* Stricta Group, which has green leaves but is not as hardy. For shady conditions, try the upright forms of yew (*Taxus baccata*), such as deep green 'Fastigiata' or the yellow 'David' and 'Standishii'.

PERFECT PARTNERS The vertical lines of an upright conifer are enhanced by contrasting mounds of foliage; its bluish-green leaves are complemented by blue flowers. **LARGE** *Ficus carica, Melianthus major, Olea europaea* **MEDIUM** *Agapanthus, Euphorbia characias, Viburnum tinus* **SMALL** *Lavandula, Nerine bowdenii*

PLANT

Always choose a strong, broad, pot to stabilize the growing plant. Use enriched potting mix, add time-release fertilizer, and soak the roots well before planting because it is important that conifers never dry out.

Avoid planting other tall plants in the same container—the shade from these other plants will result in browning of the foliage, which will not grow back. Repot after several years.

GROW

Never allow the potting mix in which your upright conifers grow to become too dry. By the time these plants turn brown, it will be too late to remedy any problems caused by lack of moisture. Add feed every week from late spring to late summer. If you grow the plant against a wall or fence, turn it regularly to both stimulate balanced growth and avoid shade damage.

Upright junipers provide striking focal points in any style of garden or patio.

MAINTAIN 'Skyrocket' is narrow and should not need training. When grown in partial shade, growth may be loose. If this happens, try tying some branches together with twine. When dry and not fed enough, the inner branches will turn brown and plants will be attacked by scale insects (see *p.37*). Do not prune into brown stems as this plant does not grow back after hard pruning.

BAY TREE *LAURUS NOBILIS*

Bay trees, the most popular evergreen for containers, are a handsome addition to any garden. Their glossy, aromatic leaves can be picked all year and used in cooking. Often chosen for their toughness and adaptability, they come in a range of shapes and sizes to suit every garden and budget.

PLANT TYPE Evergreen tree; needs protection below 23°F (–5°C)

HEIGHT Up to 9 ft 9 in (3 m) in a pot, depending on pruning and age

SPREAD Up to 6 ft 6 in (2 m) in a pot, depending on pruning and age

POT SIZE One plant per 12 in- (30 cm-) diameter pot; needs larger pot as it grows
☼ ☀

CALENDAR

	WINTER	SPRING	SUMMER	FALL
IN LEAF	▒	▒	▒	▒
IN FLOWER		▒		

COLOR

LEAVES Dark green
FLOWERS Tiny, yellow

CHOOSE

Bay trees can be bought as small plants designed for the kitchen windowsill or as tall standard plants and clipped cones. Most, however, are seedlings and show little variation in leaf shape. Never buy bay trees that seem to be dry or losing their leaves—this is a sure sign they have been neglected. *Laurus nobilis* 'Aurea' is an attractive, yellow-leaved form of the tree.

PERFECT PARTNERS Bays can be trained in a range of shapes: grown in free-form they make a great backdrop for more showy plants; trained into standards, they add height and drama. **LARGE** *Ficus carica*, *Olea europaea*, *Wisteria sinensis* **MEDIUM** *Agapanthus*, *Nerium oleander* **SMALL** *Erysimum*, *Lavandula*, *Sempervivum*

PLANT

Bay trees are often sold with their pots packed with roots and can be difficult to water. Remedy this by soaking the plant in a bucket of water for an hour before planting, which will moisten the potting mix. Plant your bay into a pot 2–4 in (5–10 cm) wider than the one you bought it in, with enriched potting mix, and add time-release fertilizer. Stake standard plants securely to prevent them from swaying or even snapping in strong winds. Do not plant 'Aurea' in hot, sunny, and dry locations or it will develop leaf scorch.

Bay trees will bring elegance and a sense of formality to a garden or patio.

GROW

Keep plants moist all year and feed with liquid fertilizer once a week from spring to fall—this is particularly important for old plants that are too big to repot. Bays do not wilt when dry, but will drop their leaves many weeks after. Starved, dry plants are also frequently attacked by scale insects (see p.37), so be sure to keep them moist to avoid this.

MAINTAIN Bays respond well to pruning. Shoots damaged by winter frost should be pruned in spring. To keep growth compact, pinch out the ends of new shoots in early summer while they are still soft. New shoots will be produced, making the plant more bushy and leafy.

Pinch out young shoots to keep plants compact and encourage further growth.

MAIDEN GRASS *MISCANTHUS SINENSIS*

These tall, elegant grasses sway in the breeze, giving dynamic movement in summer. They grow rapidly from ground level in spring, changing with the seasons. As well as their foliage value, they produce feathery plumes of flowers in fall, before the leaves turn to gold and russet shades in winter.

PLANT TYPE Hardy, herbaceous grass
HEIGHT 3 ft 3 in–8 ft 2 in (1–2.5 m) in a pot, depending on cultivar
SPREAD 2 ft 5 in–4 ft 9 in (75 cm–1.5 m) in a pot, depending on cultivar
POT SIZE One plant per 12 in- (30 cm-) diameter pot; needs larger pot as it grows
☼ ☀

CALENDAR

	WINTER	SPRING	SUMMER	FALL
IN LEAF		▒▒	▒▒▒	▒▒
IN FLOWER				▒▒

COLOR

LEAVES Green, often with white midribs; some have variegated leaves

FLOWERS Usually pinkish plumes, fading to silver

CHOOSE

Maiden grass ranges from smaller forms, 3 ft 3 in (1 m) high—including 'Gold Bar', with horizontal yellow patches on the leaves, and 'Kleine Silberspinne', with silvery flowers in fall—to giants such as 'Malepartus' 8 ft 2 in (2.5 m) high with pink flower plumes in late fall. Unless well fed and watered, all forms of silver grass will be smaller in containers than they are in the ground.

PERFECT PARTNERS Silver grass provides contrasting texture for colorful flowers. **LARGE** *Canna, Fatsia japonica* **MEDIUM** *Hydrangea, Melianthus major* **SMALL** *Begonia, Fuchsia*

PLANT

These grasses, if pot grown, can be planted all year. Any root disturbance, from digging up or dividing them, must be confined to spring. Generous, deep pots are essential for stability and to accommodate their large root system. They need organically enriched potting mix with added time-release fertilizer.

GROW

Keep silver grass weed-free and water them regularly as soon as they are in growth. As they grow through the spring and summer months they will need considerably more water. Try standing your containers in saucers during hot periods to keep the plants moist. Silver grass should not need support, but if their stems are lax it is a sign to move them to a sunnier spot. Feeding them once a week from midsummer will encourage vigorous growth. Avoid placing tall cultivars in exposed situations or the plants may be blown over by fall winds.

Variegated 'Gold Bar' has bright green leaves marked with golden bands.

The large and vigorous 'Malepartus' is at its very best in late fall.

MAINTAIN In fall, as soon as the foliage begins to turn brown, cut back your plants to half their height to reduce wind damage. In winter, check the base of the stems for snails, which like to hide among the old leaves. In spring, cut down the stems to about 4 in (10 cm) before new shoots appear. After three years, divide and repot the plants if they are becoming crowded and losing vigor.

HARDY BANANA *MUSA BASJOO*

This plant gives any patio an instant tropical look. Unlike other *Musa*, the hardy banana withstands winters and will resprout from the base, even if severe cold kills the main stems. Its huge leaves are upright at first, creating a lush canopy; established plants bloom and produce inedible fruit.

PLANT TYPE Hardy perennial; needs protection below 23°F (−5°C)
HEIGHT Up to 9 ft 9 in (3 m) in a pot
SPREAD Up to 6 ft 6 in (2 m) in a pot
POT SIZE One plant per 18 in- (45 cm-) diameter pot; needs a larger pot after two years

CALENDAR

	WINTER	SPRING	SUMMER	FALL
IN LEAF			▨	▨
IN FLOWER			▨	

COLOR

LEAVES Rich green, with an olive green "trunk"
FLOWERS Pale golden yellow

GROW

This greedy plant will amply reward your attentions. Keep it moist at all times and apply liquid fertilizer once a week in the growing season. The height of the plant is extremely dependent on how much you feed it.

MAINTAIN Remove damaged and old, yellowing leaves in summer: cut them off at their base, leaving the stem to thicken the trunk. In winter, if fall storms have damaged the leaves, cut them off at the top of the trunk.

Cover the top of small plants with fleece to prevent water getting in; wrap the trunk with fleece in very cold spells. Wrapping the pot to stop potting mix from freezing is also helpful in cold areas. Remove the fleece in mid-spring, as new foliage pushes up.

CHOOSE

The hardy or Japanese banana is a tall plant, with a long "trunk" formed from its leaf stalks; the plant produces new shoots from its base after a few years to create a clump of foliage. Its hardiness makes it the best choice for temperate gardens, but you are also likely to find other banana plants sold in garden centers during the summer.

Alternatives to the hardy banana include the smaller *M. acuminata* 'Dwarf Cavendish', which is not hardy but is great for summer pots and can be overwintered as a houseplant. Another good option is the Abyssinian banana (see *p.80*), which is similar to the hardy banana, but needs protection in winter.

PERFECT PARTNERS Bananas will dominate any plant grouping with their massive leaves and make a striking combination with other lush and imposing plants. **LARGE** *Cordyline australis, Melianthus major, Phyllostachys* **MEDIUM** *Agapanthus, Nerium oleander, Yucca* **SMALL** *Aeonium arboreum, Hosta, Lantana camara*

PLANT

This plant prefers a sunny, warm spot, but it will also be fine in a partly shaded, sheltered area. It is tall and therefore prone to being blown over in windy weather; strong winds can also split its huge paddle-shaped leaves, so avoid placing it in exposed areas. Use enriched potting mix and add time-release fertilizer. Plant your hardy banana in the summer, when the plant is actively growing and has time for the roots to fill the potting mix before winter comes.

The sail-like foliage of the hardy banana creates drama and movement.

When shoots at the base have several leaves, remove them and pot separately.

OLIVE *OLEA EUROPAEA*

The olive's distinctive airy, gray foliage gives wonderful filtered shade on a sunny day—the tree is a magnificent addition to any patio used for summer entertaining. Mild winters have emboldened people to buy them more widely, so they are now available in a range of sizes and prices.

PLANT Evergreen tree; needs protection below 23°F (−5°C)
HEIGHT Up to 9 ft 9 in (3 m) in a pot
SPREAD Up to 9 ft 9 in (3 m) in a pot
POT SIZE One plant per 12 in- (30 cm-) diameter pot

CALENDAR

	WINTER	SPRING	SUMMER	FALL
IN LEAF				
IN FLOWER				

COLOR

LEAVES Color varies from gray-green to silver
FLOWERS Small, creamy white

Tiny, scented flowers may produce small olives during a hot summer.

A large olive tree has tremendous character and is easy to look after.

CHOOSE

Older olive plants with thick trunks tend to be more cold-hardy than small, soft-stemmed plants. Also, plants with thin, silvery leaves are more resistant to cold than those with wider, greener leaves—but they are less likely to bear fruits. Small plants, grown as standards on short stems, will not grow into tall standards, so buy a plant with the trunk height you require. Over many years, the head of the plant will expand and become fuller and more bushy.

PERFECT PARTNERS

Olives are frequently trained or clipped and are perfect for formal gardens. Their gorgeous silvery leaves suit Mediterranean-style planting schemes. **LARGE** *Chamaerops humilis, Cordyline australis, Laurus nobilis* **MEDIUM** *Agapanthus, Choisya, Nerium oleander,* **SMALL** *Lavandula, Pelargonium*

PLANT

These plants love heat, sun, and good drainage, so plant them in enriched potting mix. They can be planted in any pot with drainage holes, but terra-cotta and stone look best. If planting a tall, standard plant, underplant with shrubby herbs such as thyme and rosemary. Alternatively, dress the potting mix surface with gravel or stone chippings.

GROW

Olives need watering and feeding when in growth. A high-potash fertilizer, such as tomato fertilizer, is ideal. Stop feeding in September to avoid late growth that might be damaged by winter frost. Pinch out growing tips or lightly prune in spring, and again in midsummer to keep them tidy and encourage bushiness. These evergreens must not be allowed to get dry, even in winter.

MAINTAIN Keep the trunk of standard plants clear of shoots by removing any, as they appear, in summer. In cold districts, move plants to a sheltered place: beside a sunny wall is fine, but be sure to water them. Cover the tops of small plants with fleece. Olive trees need light during the winter months, so do not store them in a garage or shed.

BAMBOO *PHYLLOSTACHYS*

These stately bamboos are ideal for bringing height, interest, and elegance to your garden all year. Young plants have thin canes; once established, they become taller and more showy. They can be invasive in the ground, but confining them to a pot keeps them under control.

PLANT TYPE Hardy, evergreen, woody grass

HEIGHT Up to 6 ft 6 in–13 ft (2–4 m) in a pot, according to species

SPREAD Up to 6 ft 6 in (2 m) in a pot, when mature

POT SIZE One plant per 12 in- (30 cm-) diameter pot; needs a larger pot as it grows

☼ ☀

CALENDAR

	WINTER	SPRING	SUMMER	FALL
IN LEAF				
IN FLOWER				

COLOR

LEAVES Green; color also introduced via canes

FLOWERS Rare

CHOOSE

With its delicate green leaves and contrasting black canes, the elegant *Phyllostachys nigra* is the most popular of all the bamboos. Another excellent choice is *P. aureosulcata* f. *aureocaulis*—its bright gold canes, streaked with green at the base, are at their most spectacular against a dark background.

The dramatic black canes of *P. nigra* are offset by the plant's green leaves.

Buy established plants; a good root system is key for healthy growth, so it is important to choose plants that are well rooted.

PERFECT PARTNERS Bamboos are perfect for Asian and minimalistic styles and contrast well with bold leaves. **LARGE** *Fatsia japonica, Laurus nobilis, Pseudopanax lessonii* **MEDIUM** *Acer palmatum, Phormium, Viburnum davidii* **SMALL** *Dryopteris erythrosora, Hakonechloa macra, Sarcococca*

PLANT

Bamboos have strong root systems that can cause pots to break if they need more room. Plastic pots will often be distorted as the rhizomes extend and may have to be cut off. Plant bamboos in spring in pots with wide tops and straight sides to make repotting easier.

Soak the root ball well before planting to ensure the plant establishes properly. Use enriched potting mix and deep pots to accommodate the roots. To avoid competition for water, do not underplant with bedding plants.

Brighten dull areas with the golden canes of *P. aureosulcata* f. *aureocaulis.*

GROW

Established, bamboos can produce canes that reach their ultimate height in one year; but this can take many years, and young plants may be shorter than anticipated. Keep plants moist and fed to ensure vigor. A general feed, rich in nitrogen, is preferable to a flowering plant food. Never let plants or leaves dry out. They tolerate wind, but strong, coastal winds will scorch the foliage. New leaves will appear in spring.

MAINTAIN Once established, cut off the tops of the canes in fall—this will ensure that they become bushier but no taller. As plants mature, remove old, thin canes, to show off the more established, thicker canes that have the best color. Trim off foliage clusters to clean off the lower parts of the canes.

PSEUDOPANAX

PSEUDOPANAX LESSONII

This striking plant from New Zealand has leathery foliage that enhances displays all year. The shrub looks more like a houseplant than anything that is grown outside, but it is relatively hardy and has unusual foliage. Small flowers appear in summer but are not as distinctive as the foliage.

PLANT TYPE Evergreen shrub; needs protection below 23°F (−5°C)
HEIGHT Up to 4 ft 9 in (1.5 m) in a pot
SPREAD Up to 3 ft 3 in (1 m) in a pot
POT SIZE One plant per 12 in- (30 cm-) diameter pot; needs a larger pot after two years
☼ ☼

CALENDAR

	WINTER	SPRING	SUMMER	FALL
IN LEAF	▨ ▨	▨ ▨	▨ ▨	▨ ▨
IN FLOWER			▨	

COLOR

LEAVES Rich green, marked with yellow
FLOWERS Green

'**Gold Splash**' looks more like a houseplant than a hardy, evergreen shrub.

CHOOSE

Pseudopanax lessonii has thick foliage that is divided into five lobes, or three on older plants. The stems are flushed with purple. The most popular cultivar 'Gold Splash', which has paler, variegated leaves that are marked with butter-yellow. Another good option is 'Moa's Toes', with dark green architectural leaves, three lobes, and an upright habit.

PERFECT PARTNERS The lush, green, and shiny foliage of the eye-catching pseudopanax is an excellent foil for flowers and plants that have fine or colorful leaves and flowers. **LARGE** *Ilex aquifolium*, *Melianthus major*, *Phormium* **MEDIUM** *Agapanthus*, *Astelia chathamica*, *Yucca* **SMALL** *Correa pulchella*, *Liriope spicata*, *Nerine bowdenii*

PLANT

Plant pseudopanax in well-drained, enriched potting mix. Avoid putting them into pots that are too big at first because they dislike wet soil, especially in winter. Small plants are less hardy than established specimens. A sheltered spot in sun is best. These are plants that thrive in coastal conditions.

GROW

Feed and water your plants moderately in spring and summer. Pinch out the growing tips in late spring and summer to encourage bushiness. If your plants become straggly, prune them in spring to produce strong new growth.

Drought and hot sun can sometimes cause the leaves of pseudopanax to become yellow and drop prematurely. If this happens, move the containers to a shady spot to recover and keep the plants moist. Clusters of inconspicuous green flowers are produced on mature, unpruned plants in summer—these will develop into clusters of small, black berries.

The tiny, green flowers of *P. lessonii* eventually mature into black berries.

MAINTAIN Young plants may need covering with fleece in cold weather; mature plants are tougher. If shoot tips are damaged by cold, trim them off, cutting back to undamaged leaves in spring. Leaves become smaller, with fewer leaflets, as the plants mature; plants can be pruned hard in spring to encourage larger leaves.

FLAMINGO WILLOW

SALIX INTEGRA 'HAKURO-NISHIKI'

The foliage of this dwarf willow is striking all summer, with pink-tinted new shoots and leaves, as bright as any flowers. It is easy to grow as long as your patio is not blazing hot in summer as this will scorch the leaves. This shrub is perfect for bringing height and color to your plant group.

PLANT TYPE Hardy, deciduous shrub
HEIGHT Up to 3 ft 3 in–6 ft 6 in (1 m–2 m) in a pot
SPREAD Up to 3 ft 3 in (1 m) in a pot
POT SIZE One plant per 12 in- (30 cm-) diameter pot; needs a larger pot as it grows

☼ ☼

CALENDAR

	WINTER	SPRING	SUMMER	FALL
IN LEAF		░░	░░	░░
IN FLOWER				

COLOR

LEAVES Bright green, spotted with white; flushed with pink when young, especially in spring
FLOWERS Insignificant

GROW

Feed weekly in spring and summer to maintain colorful new growth. If plants get dry, drop leaves, or the new growth is scorched: in hot periods, move to a part-shaded spot to prevent this. Pinch out growing tips or lightly clip the head in summer to force new, bright, growth.

CHOOSE

The flamingo willow is grafted onto a tall, bare stem to produce a lollipop-shaped plant. Its height will not increase over the years (so buy it at the height you require), but the head of foliage will become more bushy. Occasionally, shrubs are sold without the tall stem and these will make low, bushy plants.

The weeping 'Kilmarnock' willow, a cultivar of *Salix caprea*, is grafted in a similar way as the flamingo willow onto upright stems, but it has gray leaves and is particularly valued for its fluffy catkins, which appear in spring.

PERFECT PARTNERS Bright, pastel foliage complements purple, silver, and pink, while the standard shape adds formality. **LARGE** *Acer palmatum*, *Clematis* (on an obelisk), *Juniperus scopulorum* 'Skyrocket' **MEDIUM** *Agapanthus*, *Hydrangea*, *Penstemon* **SMALL** *Begonia*, *Fuchsia*, *Petunia*

PLANT

Flamingo willows are sold all year, but especially in spring. After purchase, pot in enriched potting mix. These are fast-growing and thirsty plants that must not dry out, so do not underplant them with plants that will compete for moisture. Instead, mulch the surface of the container with bark or gravel.

To encourage showy, pink, new growth, prune in spring and summer.

MAINTAIN Check for shoots appearing from below the soil or main stem: these will create green leaves and take over the plant. Such green (reverted) shoots may also appear among the variegated shoots—remove these, too. Top-dress the soil in winter or repot after a few years. Weak new growth can be caused by drought or insufficient feeding. Prune the head hard in early spring. Never cut down into the main trunk.

Flamingo willow is bushy without pruning and needs permanent staking.

WINDMILL PALM

TRACHYCARPUS FORTUNEI

This magnificent fan palm is rarely damaged by winter cold; its large, tough leaves will move and rattle in the wind. Small plants without trunks look distinctive in small pots, but the mature plants have immense impact. Striking clusters of tiny, cream flowers are produced in summer.

PLANT TYPE Hardy, evergreen tree
HEIGHT Up to 9 ft 9 in (3 m) in a pot; slow to grow and produce a trunk
SPREAD Up to 3 ft 3 in (1 m) in a pot
POT SIZE One plant per 12 in- (30 cm-) diameter pot; needs a larger pot after two years
☼ ☼

CALENDAR

	WINTER		SPRING		SUMMER		FALL	
IN LEAF								
IN FLOWER								

COLOR

LEAVES Deep green
FLOWERS Tiny but abundant, cream

GROW

Keep the potting mix moderately moist at all times. Although hardy, a sheltered position will lead to the most rapid growth. This is not a desert palm and will not withstand drying out. Feed as you do your other plants, once a week with liquid fertilizer. Growth can seem slow at first and it will take about a decade to produce a visible trunk.

MAINTAIN As the palm matures, the leaves change their position from arching to hanging. These lower, older leaves can be trimmed off to save space. Old leaves that turn yellow or brown can be cut off close to the trunk to expose the fibrous covering. When the flowers drop, cut off the old stems to keep the plant neat. Take care when doing this as the leaf stalks are thorny.

CHOOSE

Windmill palms are usually sold as seedlings with immature foliage and no trunk. The seedlings give no indication of the potential of the palm, which will produce leaves of almost 3 ft 3 in (1 m)

Windmill palms are spectacular, fully hardy plants that will live for decades.

long. Mature plants with trunks are expensive because of their age. If you are in search of a similar tree, but one that is suitable for a more exposed, windy location, try the smaller-leaved *Trachycarpus wagnerianus*.

PERFECT PARTNERS This fan palm's large leaves contrast with most plants and combine well with plants that have similar foliage. **LARGE** *Canna, Fatsia japonica, Miscanthus sinensis* **MEDIUM** *Astelia chathamica, Melianthus major, Phormium* **SMALL** *Agapanthus, Choisya, Correa pulchella*

PLANT

After purchase, pot into a slightly bigger pot, using enriched potting mix. Do not plant the top with competing plants. Pot into a bigger pot every two years. Palms transplant well, so large specimens should not be a risky purchase, even though they may be a costly one.

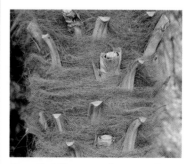

Cut off old leaves as they turn yellow to expose the fibrous trunk.

Clematis, known as the queen of climbers, is a favorite flowering plant. It is versatile, the flowers can be spectacular, and a little extra effort with training and growing will show off your talent.

FOR WALLS, FENCES, AND TRELLISES

Make the most of your vertical surfaces and add another dimension to your planting with climbing plants. Grow evergreens for a permanent screen of greenery or indulge in spectacular blooms to enhance your pots of flowers.

FAST COVER

When you need to cover walls and fences quickly, annuals are your best friends. Sweet peas grow quickly when sown in spring and you can just pop the seeds in the pots where they are to bloom. Morning glory grows just as fast, and its sky-blue flowers are remarkably beautiful, well worth the effort of replanting each year. Wisterias are known for their rapid growth, though you will have to wait a little longer for flowers. Clematis will reward you quickly, too: some produce several yards of stem in a year, and most will bloom within a few months of planting, getting better each year.

FRAGRANT BOWERS

Climbers include some of the most wonderful scents of summer. Sweet peas are popular and pretty, come in a range of colors to suit every taste, and smell divine. Roses can always be relied on for perfume as well as color and they will flower soon after planting, too. If you are prepared to wait a few years for bloom, a wisteria is a great choice and the flowers are heavily scented as well as spectacular, cascading from a pergola or down a sunny wall. The star jasmine is a plant for everyone—it is evergreen, easy to maintain, and the flowers, which open all summer, are especially fragrant in the evening, just when you want to relax in the garden and entertain friends and family.

TOWERS OF FLOWERS

Erect a trellis on a wall or wires on a fence to provide support and you can then create a backdrop of flowers. Clematis are the most popular climbers, and no wonder— there is a seemingly endless variation in colors and shapes. Summer-flowering clematis are particular favorites, with their large, star-shaped flowers, but any can be grown in pots to brighten up your outdoor space. Look also for patio climber roses, which are special small-growing roses that flower from the base to the top and throughout summer. Try them planted through metal obelisks in pots for some vertical interest, too.

CLEMATIS *CLEMATIS*

Universally adored, clematis' showy blooms bring color all through the summer. Their flowers are remarkably varied, ranging from small, nodding bells to huge, starry blooms. Generally easy to grow in sun or part shade, they can be trained across walls and fences and up obelisks.

PLANT TYPE Hardy, woody climber
HEIGHT 30 in–6 ft 6 in (75 cm–2 m) in a pot
SPREAD 24 in–3 ft 3 in (60 cm–1 m) in a pot
POT SIZE One plant per 12 in- (30 cm-) diameter pot
☼ ◑

CALENDAR

	WINTER	SPRING	SUMMER	FALL
IN LEAF				
IN FLOWER				

COLOR

LEAVES Green
FLOWERS White, pink, mauve, purple, blue, red, or yellow

CHOOSE

Clematis are divided into three main groups: spring-flowering; large-bloomed summer-flowering; and late-summer flowering. Spring-flowering kinds include *Clematis montana*, which is too large for pots, but there are also *C. alpina* and *C. macropetala* types, with their gorgeous, nodding flowers.

Large-bloomed summer-flowering clematis are the most diverse group and include several favorites such as 'Nelly Moser', with rosy lilac flowers.

The late-summer-flowering clematis include the Viticella Group, with cultivars such as 'Purpurea Plena Elegans', with purple blooms. All the Viticellas have masses of small flowers.

In addition to these three main groups, compact patio clematis are now available. Among these is the Boulevard Series, which has large flowers over a long period in summer. They include: the silvery pink FILIGREE; pale blue CHELSEA; dark blue OLYMPIA; double-flowered, purple DIAMANTINA; and the double-flowered, violet THUMBELINA. Among the non-climbing

herbaceous clematis are useful hybrids that grow to about 3 ft 3 in (1 m) high, including the indigo PETIT FAUCON, pink 'Alionushka', and lavender 'Arabella'.

PERFECT PARTNERS Clematis are ideal for clothing fences and walls behind shrubs and flowers and can be trained through and over shrubs. Compact clematis will trail over the edge of pots and through other flowers. **LARGE** *Olea europaea*, *Salix integra* 'Hakuro-nishiki', *Wisteria* **MEDIUM** *Choisya*, *Melianthus major*, *Phormium* **SMALL** *Hosta*, *Osteospermum*, *Penstemon*

Large-flowered, summer clematis bring color to sunny and shady walls.

Herbaceous clematis, such as PETIT FAUCON, are ideal for obelisks.

PLANT

Clematis can be planted at any time of year, but spring is best, just as growth is starting. They prefer cool, moist potting mix and a deep pot. Use organically enriched potting mix and plant your clematis slightly deeper than in their original pot. Water well before planting and again after to settle the potting mix.

Clematis stems are very brittle, so take care when untying them from the cane on the plant and attaching them to the new support. Choose plants with multiple stems growing from the base, if possible, as this will create a full, bushy plant more quickly. Prune back any dead and leafless stems to strong buds.

Tie new growths to supports to stop them snapping or shriveling in the wind.

When buying clematis for planting, find those with several stems at the base.

GROW

Clematis can grip supports, but it is best to tie the main shoots to the support to stop them breaking. Snails can destroy young shoots, so protect them early on (see p.37). This plant must be kept moist at all times. Dryness at the roots will cause mildew on the leaves, which starts as a powdery coating and leads to the lower leaves turning black.

Apply a time-release fertilizer in spring and then boost growth when the plants are in bloom with a liquid fertilizer weekly from midsummer on. Clematis thrive when the roots are cool; place pots of other plants in front of them for shade to keep them healthy.

In dry conditions, leaves may be coated in spores from powdery mildew.

MAINTAIN Pruning is the single most important aspect of growing clematis. Spring-flowering clematis are pruned immediately after flowering, removing some or most of the previous year's growth. The resultant new growth must be trained in place as it grows. Annual pruning is not necessary.

Large-bloomed summer-flowering clematis are pruned in spring but only cut back by about half, to a pair of strong, fat buds. If they are pruned hard, which may be necessary with neglected, tangled plants, they will not flower the summer after pruning.

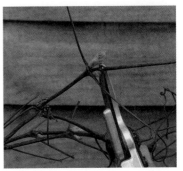

In spring, prune large-flowered clematis back to strong growth buds.

Late-flowering kinds are pruned hard in spring, to about 8 in (20 cm) to promote growth from low down as they produce long stems with flowers on the ends.

Modern, patio clematis are pruned hard every spring and will flower in summer and into fall. Herbaceous clematis flower on the stems produced from the base the same year and are cut back close to the ground in spring.

Clematis do not need protection from the cold but must be kept moist.

Large-bloomed clematis are prone to clematis wilt disease, which causes the stems to wither and the leaves to blacken. It only affects shoots above soil level, so planting clematis deeply—ensuring there are buried, dormant buds—allows the plant to resprout and bloom again. Other types of clematis are not affected by this disease.

If shoots are not tied in and properly supported, they may suddenly shrivel.

PERSIAN IVY *HEDERA COLCHICA*

This bold-leaved ivy thrives in most situations, is far more impressive than the common ivy, and invaluable in winter. Like all ivies, it can flower and produce black berries that are useful for wildlife. With stems that attach to supports using aerial roots, it is ideal for growing up walls.

PLANT TYPE Self-clinging, hardy, evergreen climber

HEIGHT 9 ft 9 in (3 m) in a pot, more when the plant is mature

SPREAD 9 ft 9 in (3 m) in a pot, more when the plant is mature

POT SIZE One plant per 12 in- (30 cm-) diameter pot; needs a larger pot after a few years

☼ ☼ ☼

CALENDAR

	WINTER	SPRING	SUMMER	FALL
IN LEAF				
IN FLOWER				

COLOR

LEAVES Dark green, often variegated

FLOWERS Small and greenish yellow; black berries

GROW

For the best results, keep this ivy evenly moist and do not allow it to dry out. This is important in winter, when the dense foliage may prevent rain from reaching the pot. Feed your plant once a week, unless using time-release fertilizer in spring, in which case, it will not need liquid fertilizer.

MAINTAIN Prune regularly between winter and midsummer to restrict size and make the plant bushy. Plants can produce all-green shoots, which should be cut out. Check for scale insects (see p.37) on mature plants; walls and fences can be a hiding place for snails in winter.

Persian ivy's variegated leaves brighten even the darkest walls and fences.

CHOOSE

This large ivy is most often grown in the form of variegated cultivars. 'Dentata Variegata', with butter-yellow edges, is the most popular. 'Sulphur Heart' can be spectacular, with bright yellow centers to its green-edged leaves. Both have leaves that can be 8 in (20 cm) long and 6 in (15 cm) wide. Sometimes plants grow as much as 24 in (60 cm) a year but can be contained with regular pruning.

In mild areas, try *Hedera algeriensis* 'Gloire de Marengo', if you want a faster climber. Its leaves are a mix of green, gray, and cream with red leaf stalks.

PERFECT PARTNERS Persian ivy's large, glossy leaves make a lush backdrop to other evergreens and bright flowers. **LARGE** *Acer palmatum, Musa basjoo, Phyllostachys* **MEDIUM** *Buxus sempervirens, Camellia, Viburnum davidii* **SMALL** *Dryopteris erythrosora, Fuchsia* (trailing), *Hosta*

PLANT

Ivy clings to any surface, so think how you will move the container or repot the plant before planting. It can be grown up a freestanding support and, since it tolerates pruning, can be trained in various ways. Plant in enriched potting mix, untie from the cane you bought it on, and wind the stems around the base of the support so that new growth can be placed as you wish.

Prune ivy regularly through the year to keep its shoots out of gutters and tiles.

CLIMBING HYDRANGEA

HYDRANGEA ANOMALA SUBSP. *PETIOLARIS*

This is a classic shade climber. In spring, its fresh leaves are bright green and it produces delicate, lacy flowers. In fall, the leaves change to a buttery yellow before they fall and the old flowers become pale brown, providing winter texture.

PLANT TYPE Hardy, woody climber; sticks to walls and fences with aerial roots.
HEIGHT 6 ft 6 in (2 m), or more, in a pot
SPREAD 6 ft 6 in (2 m), or more, in a pot
POT SIZE One plant per 12 in- (30 cm-) diameter pot; needs a larger pot after a few years

CALENDAR

	WINTER	SPRING	SUMMER	FALL
IN LEAF				
IN FLOWER				

COLOR

LEAVES Bright green, butter-yellow in fall
FLOWERS Creamy white

season and will make new shoots up to 24 in (60 cm) long each season. These must be tied to the support at first as they grow until they attach themselves.

MAINTAIN Once the plant has produced two or three years of climbing stems it will start to bloom. Flowers appear on short shoots that grow at right angles away from the climbing stems. Do not prune these off because they will flower for several years. Prune in summer or winter to reduce height. The plant will need repotting until it is in the biggest pot you can manage; keep it healthy by top-dressing in spring (see *p.31*).

Climbing hydrangea is a slow starter, but will eventually cover large areas.

CHOOSE

With its attractive, heart-shaped foliage and clusters of eye-catching, creamy white flowers, this vigorous and hardy climbing hydrangea is the perfect choice for covering walls and fences. There are brighter cultivars, such as 'Miranda', with yellow-edged leaves in summer.

PERFECT PARTNERS The climbing hydrangea's delicate, white flowers are offset by pale green neighbors and elegant foliage. **LARGE** *Clematis, Hedera colchica, Phyllostachys* **MEDIUM** *Camellia, Euonymus fortunei, Viburnum* **SMALL** *Heuchera, Hosta, Vinca major*

PLANT

The climbing hydrangea clings to supports with aerial roots produced by its stems. It will therefore stick to walls and fences (repotting will be difficult if it attaches to a wall). It will also happily grow up a wooden obelisk or trellis. Plant in an enriched potting mix and keep moist. Untie the plant from its cane and lay the stems horizontally at the base of the support so that new growth produces a bushy plant.

GROW

This plant is a slow starter, but keep it watered and feed once a week in the growing season—and do not give up. It should start to climb in the second

Roots that grow from stems allow the plant to grab onto any support.

MORNING GLORY

IPOMOEA TRICOLOR

The flowers of this fast-growing annual climber are large and intensely sky-blue. Each flower lasts just a day, opening in the morning and closing by afternoon, later on cloudy days. Once it starts to bloom, it continues for months, with a fresh crop of glorious blooms each morning.

PLANT TYPE Frost-tender, annual climber. Does not stick to walls or fences—needs tying to supports or canes with string, wire, or similar. Needs protection below 41°F (5°C)

HEIGHT Up to 6 ft 6 in (2 m) in a pot

SPREAD Up to 3 ft 3 in (1 m) in a pot

POT SIZE Three plants per 12 in- (30 cm-) diameter pot

CALENDAR

	WINTER	SPRING	SUMMER	FALL
IN LEAF				
IN FLOWER				

COLOR

LEAVES Light green, heart-shaped

FLOWERS Pure, light blue flowers with white centers

Seedlings are sensitive to cold and need a sunny, warm spot to thrive.

CHOOSE

Ipomoea tricolor, the common, blue morning glory, is the most popular variety of this plant. With its lush foliage and glorious, trumpet-shaped blooms, it has immense charm and is ideal for walls and fences.

However, if you are in search of a similar plant in a different color, try 'Crimson Rambler', with beautiful, cherry-red and white flowers, or 'Grandpa Ott', which has purple flowers, is less cold-sensitive, and sometimes self-seeds. The more vigorous *I. alba* has large, white, scented, nocturnal flowers.

PERFECT PARTNERS Morning glory's eye-catching, blue flowers contrast with gray and yellow foliage and blooms. **LARGE** *Canna, Clematis, Laurus nobilis* **MEDIUM** *Euphorbia characias, Melianthus major, Nerium oleander* **SMALL** *Fuchsia, Lantana camara, Osteospermum*

PLANT

Morning glory is easily grown from seed and flowers within three months. To encourage germination, soak the seeds overnight in water before sowing. Sow two seeds per 3 in (8 cm) pot of fresh potting mix, about ½ in (1 cm) deep. Keep in a warm propagator at around 68°F (20°C). Seedlings should appear within three weeks. Avoid overwatering and cold temperatures, which cause leaf yellowing and new growth to be white.

GROW

When about 12 in (30 cm) high, the seedlings will need a cane for support. They can be planted into pots once the last frost has passed. Morning glory needs a moist, rich soil and warmth to flourish, so plant in pots of fresh potting mix on a warm, sheltered patio. When established, they rapidly grow and twine up their support. They have to grow quite tall with their main stems before they begin to bloom.

MAINTAIN Pinch out growing tips of the main shoots before they reach the extent of their canes or trellis. This will encourage bushiness and flowers. Feed every week with a high-potash fertilizer and keep the plants moist at all times. The previous day's flowers usually drop the following day, so deadheading is rarely necessary.

Every morning is greeted by a fresh flush of magnificent, intense blue flowers.

SWEET PEA *LATHYRUS ODORATUS*

One of the true glories of summer, sweet peas are simple to grow and have a magnificent perfume. They are also great to cut as fresh flowers for the home. There are many types, ranging from dwarf kinds, suitable for hanging baskets, to tall climbers perfect for walls, fences, trellises, and obelisks.

PLANT TYPE Hardy, annual climber; may need tying to supports or canes with string, wire, or similar

HEIGHT Up to 6 ft 6 in (2 m) in a pot

SPREAD Up to 24 in (60 cm) in a pot

POT SIZE Three plants per 12 in- (30 cm-) diameter pot; can be planted in larger pots with other annuals

CALENDAR

	WINTER	SPRING	SUMMER	FALL
IN LEAF				
IN FLOWER				

COLOR

LEAVES Grayish green

FLOWERS White, cream, pink, red, purple (almost black), lavender-blue (not true blue)

Seedlings should be kept in a cool, bright spot to ensure health and vigor.

Keep picking the blooms of sweet peas as they open to encourage growth.

CHOOSE

The best sweet peas for containers are the old Grandiflora types, which have compact growth; small leaves; and small, highly fragrant flowers. They include 'Cupani', 'Matucana', and 'Painted Lady'.

The large-flowered Spencer types are taller and less easy to keep on an obelisk, although their long-stemmed flowers are better for cutting. Do not confuse them with the perennial pea (*Lathyrus latifolius*), which is unscented.

PERFECT PARTNERS Plant sweet peas through shrubs and up walls, fences, and trellises to add splashes of color and perfume. **LARGE** *Clematis, Rosa* (climbing), *Trachelospermum jasminoides* **MEDIUM** *Canna, Nerium oleander, Olea europaea* **SMALL** *Alstroemeria, Heliotropium arborescens, Petunia*

PLANT

Sweet peas are hardy, but it is usual to start the plants in a greenhouse or on a windowsill. Although seeds can be sown in fall, it is easiest to sow in spring. It helps germination if you scrape the seed coat on the opposite side of the seed from the "eye." Then sow two or three seeds per 3 in (8 cm) pot, about ½ in (1 cm) deep. Keep moist and above 50°F (10°C). Germination takes two to three weeks.

GROW

When seedlings have four or five leaves, pinch out the growing tip. This encourages low branching and greater vigor. When these side shoots are 3 in (8 cm) long they can be planted out; they will survive light frosts. They may need tying to supports at first but soon the tendrils will grab hold and they will need less attention. Keep moist and feed once a week. Watch for aphids, which attack shoots and spread viruses.

MAINTAIN Keeping plants moist is key. If they dry out they will drop flower buds and develop mildew (see p.37). Always remove dead flowers. If seed pods set, the plants stop growing and flowering. Pick as many flowers as you like, but only when they are fully open: sweet-pea flower buds do not open if picked. At the end of the season, allow a few pods to form to set some seeds that you can sow next year.

ROSE *ROSA*

These classic plants, with their dainty foliage and delightful flowers, will bring beauty, color, and scent to your garden. They bloom from summer to fall and their height helps disguise walls and fences. The recently introduced patio climbers are compact and easy to care for.

PLANT TYPE Hardy, deciduous shrub
HEIGHT 3 ft 3 in–6 ft 6 in (1–2 m) in a pot
SPREAD 24 in–6 ft 6 in (60 cm–2 m) in a pot
POT SIZE One plant per 12 in- (30 cm-) diameter pot

CALENDAR

	WINTER	SPRING	SUMMER	FALL
IN LEAF				
IN FLOWER				

COLOR

LEAVES Deep green
FLOWERS White, pink, red, orange, yellow, or purple

GRAHAM THOMAS is a tall rose with large, full, fragrant blooms.

CHOOSE

Traditional climbing roses and ramblers tend to grow tall and have bare lower branches. While this is fine at the back of a garden border, where other plants can conceal their leafless stems, it is not ideal in pots on a patio. So, if you are looking for roses for fences, walls, trellises, or containers, choose patio climbers, which have small but plentiful leaves and flowers and are also ideal when space is an issue.

True patio climbers include golden LAURA FORD, orange WARM WELCOME, red LOVE KNOT and pink OPEN ARMS. ONWARD AND UPWARD has salmon-pink flowers. These plants all reach about 6 ft 6 in (2 m) high and 2 ft (60 cm) wide and have a little scent. PINK SKYLINER has masses of soft pink flowers on flexible stems and flowers profusely, though there is minimal fragrance.

Tall bush roses are also great for covering walls and fences, since the one-sided light source will naturally "stretch" their growth. The ever-popular RHAPSODY IN BLUE and yellow GRAHAM THOMAS are perfect for this. The disease-resistant PINK FLOWER CARPET produces long stems and can be trained as a small climber.

PERFECT PARTNERS Roses are heavy feeders, so they grow best in their own containers. Place these among a wide variety of other plants, wherever a splash of summer color needs to be introduced. Slender climbing roses can be trained up tall shrubs. **LARGE** *Clematis, Laurus nobilis, Olea europaea* **MEDIUM** *Alstroemeria, Hemerocallis, Lavandula* **SMALL** *Festuca glauca, Hosta, Petunia*

RHAPSODY IN BLUE is a bush rose that can be trained as a small climber. Its unusual color and pronounced perfume make it a popular choice.

PLANT

Roses need a rich soil, so plant them in enriched potting mix. They can be planted all year if pot-grown, but winter or spring is best. Bare-root specimens can be planted from late fall to early spring, when dormant, but they must be planted as soon as they are received. Roses are budded onto rootstocks and the "join" should be at about soil level. Mycorrhizal fungi (beneficial fungi, available in small packs), sprinkled onto roots at planting time, improves growth and establishment. After planting, prune back any badly placed or broken stems and thin, twiggy growths.

Roses prefer a sunny spot, though some shade throughout the day will not harm them. An open site, with good air circulation, will reduce fungal diseases.

PINK FLOWER CARPET is easy to grow and loves a sunny spot.

GROW

The key to keeping roses strong and healthy is to feed them. Apply a dressing of rose fertilizer to the pots in spring and then feed them with liquid fertilizer every week all summer.

Most modern roses are resistant to disease, but if blackspot appears on the leaves, spray regularly with fungicide to prevent further leaf infection. If left untreated, this disease will cause premature leaf drop and weaken the plant. Blackspot is less troublesome if plants are healthy and well fed.

After pruning your roses in spring, new shoots will grow and then flower in summer. When they have flowered, cut back the shoot to the topmost full leaf. This will keep the plant neat and promote new growth and flowers. Train strong, new shoots up the support. These will bloom the following year and may have flowers at the ends of the shoots during the first year.

If left untreated, blackspot can severely weaken rose bushes.

Aphids often infest the new shoots (see p.36)—rubbing them off should keep them under control.

MAINTAIN Pruning is key to neat and healthy plants. Do this in spring, just as the new growth is starting. The aim is to remove old, twiggy growth and keep air moving through the plant. Cut off thin, twiggy shoots at their base and prune away dead stems. Shorten long stems and tie them into the supports. Cut out any old, woody stems. In winter, keep the potting mix moist and check all ties are secure to prevent winter gales from damaging the stems.

After a few years, your rose may need to be put into a larger pot: always use enriched potting mix. If the plant is too big to repot, remove some of the mix from the surface of the pot and replace with fresh potting mix.

Pruning your roses is key to keeping them healthy, neat, and in great condition.

STAR JASMINE

TRACHELOSPERMUM JASMINOIDES

Star jasmine is one of the few evergreen, flowering climbers; it is also wonderfully fragrant, compact, and easily trained. Its flowers are produced for many months throughout summer and a few leaves turn red in fall, making it a great choice for year-round interest in a sunny spot.

PLANT TYPE Hardy, evergreen climber; needs a sheltered position and will not tolerate cold, exposed sites

HEIGHT Up to 6 ft 6 in (2 m) in a pot

SPREAD Up to 6 ft 6 in (2 m) in a pot

POT SIZE One plant per 12 in- (30 cm-) diameter pot; needs a larger pot as it matures

CALENDAR

	WINTER	SPRING	SUMMER	FALL
IN LEAF				
IN FLOWER				

COLOR

LEAVES Glossy, dark green
FLOWERS White or cream

This plant will not need deadheading, but remove old flowers in late summer.

CHOOSE

In its common form, this attractive, evergreen climber produces white or cream flowers, which are at their most fragrant at night. The cultivar STAR OF TOSCANA has flowers that open cream but change to gold, while 'Variegatum' has leaves marbled in white, but is slow-growing. Another option, with masses of pink flowers in summer, is 'Pink Showers'—a recent form of the species *Trachelospermum asiaticum*.

PERFECT PARTNERS Star jasmine's dark leaves are an excellent foil for almost any plant. **LARGE** *Musa basjoo, Olea europaea, Pseudopanax lessonii* **MEDIUM** *Correa pulchella, Melianthus major, Phormium* **SMALL** *Dianthus, Erysimum, Pelargonium*

PLANT

Star jasmine prefers a sunny, sheltered site. It dislikes wet soil, so make sure its pot is not too big, especially when small. If buying plug plants or young plants in pots that are smaller than 4 in (10 cm) in diameter, pot into a slightly bigger pot for a year to grow on. Larger plants, 24 in (60 cm) or more tall, can be potted into 12 in (30 cm) pots. Use enriched potting mix. Keep moist, especially in winter, but never waterlogged.

Star jasmine will grow beautifully on its own against a sunny wall, fence, or trellis.

GROW

Keep in a sunny location. Small plants are more sensitive to cold than large plants and may benefit from a fleece in their first winter. Water freely in spring and summer and feed with a high-potash fertilizer once a week. This plant has twining stems and may need help to grab supports at first. Train it so the shoots spread out and give good cover of the support.

MAINTAIN Star jasmine branches out freely when pruned. Light pruning in spring to shape it and remove any winter-cold damage; this will not affect flowering. The plant will drop leaves if you allow it to dry out.

WISTERIA _WISTERIA SINENSIS_

This is the most impressive of all hardy climbers. It is fast-growing and spectacular, with cascades of fragrant blooms. Although potentially huge, with careful pruning, its size can be limited when grown in a pot. Be patient and methodical in this task and you will be well-rewarded.

PLANT TYPE Hardy, deciduous, woody climber

HEIGHT 9 ft 9 in (3 m) in a pot, depending on pruning

SPREAD 9 ft 9 in (3 m) in a pot, depending on pruning

POT SIZE One plant per 12 in- (30 cm-) diameter pot; needs a larger pot after a few years

 ☀

CALENDAR

	WINTER	SPRING	SUMMER	FALL
IN LEAF				
IN FLOWER				

COLOR

LEAVES Green in summer, bright yellow in fall

FLOWERS Lavender/mauve; others have purple, pink, or white

Once established, wisteria can grow as much as 3 ft 3 in (1 m) in a year.

CHOOSE

With its magnificent, perfumed blooms this hardy climber is an excellent choice for covering walls and fences. There are numerous cultivars to choose from; of these, 'Prolific' is one of the best as it flowers freely and is highly fragrant.

If you prefer a wisteria with longer and less densely packed flower clusters, try _Wisteria floribunda_. 'Multijuga' is this species' most impressive cultivar, with flowers hanging almost 3 ft 3 in (1 m) long, while 'Yae-Kokuryu' has double purple and white flowers. However, avoid buying any plant that is simply labeled as "wisteria" as these can often turn out to be poor seedlings.

PERFECT PARTNERS Wisteria forms a great backdrop to many other plants. **LARGE** _Cordyline australis_, _Olea europaea_, _Salix integra_ 'Hakuro-nishiki' **MEDIUM** _Euphorbia_, _Ficus carica_, _Phormium_ **SMALL** _Alstroemeria_, _Dianthus_

PLANT

Consider how to train and grow your wisteria. You can train them as standards, with a single stem and a head of growth, but they will need a stout stake. Plant in a large pot in enriched potting mix. Remove any shoots below the graft point (a bulge on the stem, where the plant was grafted to the rootstock).

GROW

Prune out any dead stems and any that are growing awkwardly. If planting against a wall, spread out the shoots horizontally to spread the growth at the base. If growing as a standard, tie the stems to a stake. Wisterias are thirsty plants in summer and require frequent watering. Feed once a week when in growth. After a few years, they need potting into a bigger pot.

MAINTAIN Pruning is the secret to getting your wisteria to bloom. A young plant will fling out long growths and these should be pruned in August. By this time they can be very long, so you can shorten them slightly earlier in summer. Then prune again, back to four leaves, in August. This will control growth and encourage flowers. If necessary, these pruned shoots can then be cut back again, this time to two buds, in winter. If this pruning is done every year, the plant may start to bloom in three or four years.

Regular pruning is the key to success with the hardy and vigorous wisteria.

Brighten up dull walls and fences with hanging baskets brimming with colorful blooms. Considered an essential part of summer, with imagination and the right choice of plants, they can become a year-long feature.

FOR BASKETS, BOXES, AND PLANTERS

If you cannot wait for climbers to cover walls and fences with color, then hanging baskets, wall planters, and window boxes are the answer—a terrific way to bring interest and vibrant color to even the dullest area of your garden.

CASCADES OF BLOOM

When filling baskets with plants, you need something colorful, and spectacular—nothing fits the bill better than petunias. Recent advances in breeding have made these stalwarts of the garden and patio far easier to look after: now resistant to disease and less prone to damage in wet weather, they keep their good looks longer. The color range has expanded, too, with combinations that include black flowers, spotted petals, and even green-edged blooms. Also look out for the special trailing kinds that will form great sheets of blooms. On a smaller scale, try calibrachoas—the plants and flowers are not as big, but they still pack a floral punch with nonstop displays of pretty blooms, until halted by the first frost of fall.

TRADITIONAL FAVORITES

If you want a display just like your grandma had, you probably need to plant fuchsias. These old-fashioned favorites have pendulous blooms in a wide range of colors and shapes and are great for beginners: they are easy to grow but, with a bit of extra effort, can be spectacular. Trailing fuchsias show off their luscious blooms to perfection in baskets and planters. The ideal partners for fuchsias are lobelias, most often seen in rich blue (the only color not found in fuchsias). Their mass of sparkling flowers cascading from baskets is a common sight; easy to care for and tolerant of some shade, they are deservedly popular.

BRIGHTENING SHADY WALLS

Never let a shady wall prevent you from planting a colorful display—many plants thrive with very little direct sun. Both fuchsias and begonias, for example, will grow and flower well with sun for just half the day. Modern begonias become fountains of blooms and are easy to please—their fabulous array of colors will bring light or rich colors to your planters. Don't forget about colorful foliage either. Pop in a few small plants of golden creeping Jenny or variegated ground ivy and their long trails of growth will sway in the wind and bring vertical interest and a more balanced display.

TRAILING BEGONIA *BEGONIA*

Begonias are variable plants with a wide range of habits and colors. Flowers can be dainty or large and voluptuous. Trailing begonias usually produce tubers but can also be grown from seed and bought already in bloom. They thrive in sun or part shade and flower continuously in summer.

PLANT TYPE Half-hardy perennial grown as half-hardy annual; needs protection below 41°F (5°C)

HEIGHT Up to 12in (30cm) in a pot, trailing to 8in (20cm)

SPREAD Up to 12in (30cm) in a pot

POT SIZE One plant per 12in- (30cm-) diameter pot; three plants per 16in- (40cm-) diameter pot
☼ ☼

CALENDAR

	WINTER	SPRING	SUMMER	FALL
IN LEAF				
IN FLOWER				

COLOR

LEAVES Usually dark green, sometimes flushed with purple and brown

FLOWERS White, cream, yellow, orange, red, pink, or multicolored

Whether trailing from baskets or planters, begonias thrive in sun or shade.

CHOOSE

Trailing begonias grown from seed or tubers usually have thick, fleshy stems and large, spectacular flowers. The newer kinds that are based on *Begonia boliviensis*, such as the Starshine Series and Million Kisses Series, have more delicate foliage and masses of slender-petaled blooms. *B. sutherlandii* is a an orange-flowered species with pale green foliage, often veined with red, that creates a wonderful display.

PERFECT PARTNERS Begonias are happy in shade as well as sun, so they mix well with shade lovers, unlike most other bedding plants, which require full sun. **LARGE** *Canna, Clematis, Pseudopanax lessonii* **MEDIUM** *Euonymus fortunei, Hemerocallis* **SMALL** *Hakonechloa macra, Pelargonium, Verbena*

PLANT

Start your trailing begonia tubers indoors, either in a propagator or on a sunny windowsill during the early spring. Water them sparingly until they are in full growth.

Seedling plug plants should also be grown on indoors—take care not to overwater them. Grow them on in a temperature of more than 60°F (15°C). Larger trailing begonia plants can be bought in late spring for direct planting in pots and baskets, but it is essential that they are protected from frost and from cold temperatures.

B. sutherlandii is a dainty gem. You can save its bulbils to plant for the next year.

GROW

Be careful not to water begonias too much when they are small: cold, wet potting mix will lead to root rot and plants collapsing. Although the growth of begonias will cascade, they are upright at first, so they should be planted in the center of containers rather than around the edge. Once established and thriving, water and feed well to ensure healthy growth and flowers. If allowed to dry out, they are prone to mildew.

MAINTAIN The large flowers of begonias drop and can make a mess of paving, so will need collecting. The female flowers also produce triangular seed pods, which should be removed. Old flowers falling onto lower leaves can sometimes cause rot in cooler, wetter conditions during fall. When fall frosts kill off the foliage, the tubers of some kinds of begonias can be saved, dried, and kept to grow the following year.

MILLION BELLS *CALIBRACHOA*

A recent arrival to our gardens is million bells, bred for containers. They are bushy, with small leaves and an endless display of bright, trumpet-shaped flowers, like tiny petunias. Their color range is now vast and there are also double kinds, with flowers that resemble miniature roses.

PLANT TYPE Half-hardy perennial grown as a half-hardy annual; needs protection below 41°F (5°C)

HEIGHT Up to 10 in (25 cm) in a pot, sometimes trailing to 8 in (20 cm)

SPREAD Up to 12 in (30 cm) in a pot

POT SIZE Three plants per 12 in- (30 cm-) diameter pot, five plants per 16 in- (40 cm-) diameter pot

CALENDAR

	WINTER	SPRING	SUMMER	FALL
IN LEAF		▓▓	▓▓	▓
IN FLOWER		▓▓	▓▓	▓

COLOR

LEAVES Small, mid-green; stems can be red-flushed

FLOWERS White, pink, red, lilac, purple, yellow, orange, almost black, or multicolored

GROW

Pinch out the tips of straggly shoots when the plants are young to make them more bushy. Make sure stronger growing plants do not smother young plants, which can be slow to get established. If planting in baskets, allow the plants to get established before hanging them in their final positions—this will avoid damage by strong winds.

MAINTAIN Million bells are neat and bushy and do not set seeds so may not need deadheading. It is worth removing the dead flowers of double kinds, which can look unsightly. Feed weekly with liquid fertilizer throughout the summer to stimulate new growth and flowers. Keep well watered when plants are mature to prevent mildew, which can sometimes attack dry plants.

Compact and covered in blooms, million bells is perfect for hanging baskets.

CHOOSE

Plant breeders have been working hard in recent years to introduce new varieties of million bells, and they are changing all the time.

The latest developments include double flowers and new colors such as pastel shades, contrasting veins in the flowers, and eye-catching, almost black blooms. In addition, the new varieties have an improved resistance to cold temperatures and alkaline soils, which were problems with the older kinds.

PERFECT PARTNERS Million bells cover themselves with blooms, so it is best to combine them with similar bright, bold companions or they will steal the show. **LARGE** *Cordyline australis*, *Olea europaea* **MEDIUM** *Dahlia*, *Penstemon* **SMALL** *Dianthus*, *Heuchera*, *Pelargonium*

PLANT

Million bells are usually small and straggly when they are young, giving you no indication whatsoever of the tremendous mounds of color that they will eventually create. But they are sensitive to cold and wet potting mix when small, which results in a yellowing of the leaves and, eventually, root rot.

Wait until the weather is warm before putting your million bells into group plantings or on their own. Make sure they are well rooted in their pots before planting. Water them carefully at first to avoid cold, wet potting mix around the roots.

These plants do not set seeds, so deadheading is for aesthetic reasons only.

TRAILING FUCHSIA *FUCHSIA*

These plants are a traditional feature of summer gardens. Tumbling from baskets and window boxes, they combine elegance and a rainbow of colors in their beautiful flowers. Large, frilly, double blooms are the most popular choice, but many glorious smaller, single flowers are also available.

PLANT TYPE Half-hardy perennial; needs protection below 41°F (5°C)
HEIGHT 12 in (30 cm), some trailing to 12 in (30 cm)
SPREAD 18 in (45 cm)
POT SIZE One to three plants per 12-in- (30-cm-) diameter pot
☼ ☀

CALENDAR

	WINTER	SPRING	SUMMER	FALL
IN LEAF				
IN FLOWER				

COLOR

LEAVES Green, often flushed with red, often variegated
FLOWERS Red, white, pink, purple, lilac, or orange: often bicolored

CHOOSE

Perfect for partly shaded areas, fuchsias flower all summer and add sparkle to a garden or patio. The four main kinds of fuchsia are trailing, climbing, upright, and standard. There are no hardy trailing fuchsias, but a few of the erect, hardy kinds, such as 'Garden News', have a lax habit and double flowers.

Trailing fuchsias are half hardy, and those grown in containers are more sensitive to cold winter weather than those in the ground. They have weak stems, so their growth cascades from pots—and there is a wealth of these spectacular flowers to choose from.

The double-flowered kinds include red and white 'Swingtime', pale pink and white 'Devonshire Dumpling', pink and purple 'Taffeta Bow', pink and white 'Happy Wedding Day', and orange and red 'Orange King'.

Fuchsias with smaller, single blooms also cascade. The most popular include coral-pink 'Jack Shahan', white and purple 'Nora' (Bella Series), the white and lilac 'Waveney Gem', as well as the white and purple 'Auntie Jinks'. 'Autumnale' is a terrific cultivar with red and gold leaves and dark red flowers.

PERFECT PARTNERS Fuchsias are flamboyant—mix them with other bright flowers or use them to bring glamour to groups of colored foliage. **LARGE** *Cordyline australis*, *Nerium oleander*, *Salix integra* 'Hakuro-nishiki' **MEDIUM** *Dahlia*, *Hosta*, *Lilium* **SMALL** *Begonia*, *Lobelia* (trailing), *Petunia*

With careful watering and feeding, your container will drip with fuchsias, as in this gorgeous basket of 'Orange King'.

'Auntie Jinks' is an old favorite with small flowers, but masses of them.

PLANT

Fuchsias are sold in spring and summer and can be bought as small plants in 3 in (8 cm) pots, or similar, or as smaller, plug plants. The plug plants are tender and soft and need careful growing on in bright, frost-free conditions before they are ready to plant out. Young fuchsias can easily be damaged by frost and must not be planted out before the danger of late spring frost has passed. Pinch out the growing tips of the plants to make them bushy. More stems mean later flowers, but many more of them.

If you are growing trailing fuchsias in containers for a single summer, they can be planted in commercial potting mix, with or without organic enrichment.

Trailing fuchsias are perfect for hanging baskets, creating mounds of growth and pendant flowers. Large plants quickly fill their space and produce masses of flowers.

GROW

Keep trailing fuchsias moist at all times and feed them once a week in summer and fall. It is important to remove any dead flowers as the plants grow. Flowers tend to drop off as they fade, but the seed pods remain on the plant. These should be pinched off immediately or they will mature and ripen—when this happens, plants tend not to produce more flowers. The berries, if left to ripen, are edible. Aphids often attack shoots and should be sprayed or rubbed off (see p.36).

MAINTAIN In wet weather, rust disease can be a problem: the leaves develop orange spots and drop prematurely. Spraying with a fungicide will prevent any further damage, but removing affected leaves and pruning the plants to improve air circulation can reduce existing damage.

In hot weather, capsid bugs may feed on the young shoots, causing ragged holes in the upper leaves: pinch out the growing tips to remove this damage. Flowering is usually not affected.

Keep trailing fuchsias blooming by removing seed pods when flowers drop.

Vine-weevil grubs can also eat the roots and may cause your fuchsia plants to suddenly wilt and fail (see p.36).

In fall, after the first frost, plants need frost protection. They will drop their leaves but are never completely dormant and must be kept moist in winter. It may be possible to maintain plants until the next year by trimming them back lightly and covering with fleece. Moving them near the house can give them the protection they need. Alternatively, plants can be trimmed back, dug up, and stored in trays or boxes of potting mix, or in composted bark, and kept barely moist.

It is also possible to keep plants over winter as young plants. Cuttings root easily and can be taken in spring or late summer; keep these small, young plants on a sunny, cool windowsill over winter..

Fuchsia cuttings, taken in spring or late summer, will root in potting mix or water.

VARIEGATED GROUND IVY

GLECHOMA HEDERACEA 'VARIEGATA'

Grown mainly for its foliage, this useful trailer mixes well with other plants and has attractive, lavender flowers. Small plants present cascades of scalloped leaves in a few months. Fully hardy, it can be used in winter as well as in summer.

PLANT TYPE Hardy perennial; survives frost but is usually grown as an annual

HEIGHT Up to 2 in (5 cm) in a pot, trailing to 3 ft 3 in (1 m)

SPREAD Up to 8 in (20 cm) in a pot, when trailing; up to 24 in (60 cm) as ground cover

POT SIZE Three plants per 12 in- (30 cm-) diameter pot; usually combined with other plants

☼ ☀

CALENDAR

	WINTER	SPRING	SUMMER	FALL
IN LEAF				
IN FLOWER				

COLOR

LEAVES Gray-green with white edges

FLOWERS Lavender

The gray-green and white leaves of this ivy offset pink and lilac flowers.

This plant's dainty leaves will cascade from baskets and planters.

CHOOSE

Variegated ground ivy, often sold under the name *Nepeta*, is a quick-growing, tough, frost-hardy plant that is great in pots, hanging baskets, and window boxes. It creates cascades of dainty leaves throughout the year. Two recent cultivars are 'Dappled Light' with yellow-speckled foliage and 'Rapunzel' with yellow-edged leaves. *Ajuga reptans* is similar, but has glossy leaves, in a variety of colors, and spikes of lavender flowers. It is evergreen and particularly useful for winter displays.

PERFECT PARTNERS Variegated ground ivy's gray-green, white-edged leaves mix well with silver foliage and pink summer flowers. **LARGE** *Acer palmatum, Clematis, Salix integra* 'Hakuro-nishiki' **MEDIUM** *Camellia, Lilium, Viburnum* **SMALL** *Carex, Euonymus, Hosta*

PLANT

Plants are available in spring either as plug plants or young, potted plants. Plug plants are useful for hanging baskets, where they can be put around the edge to trail down. Larger plants are good to cover the soil in larger pots and trail over the edge. Although this is a hardy plant, young plants may have been grown under cover for sale and their soft young shoots may be damaged by frost, so protect them when young.

GROW

Pinch out growing tips when the plants are young to encourage them to branch, or push the stems into the soil surface, where they will root: this gives them more vigor and result in bushier growth. Keep plants watered and fed. They do not respond well to drying out—if short of water, they will lose their older leaves, become straggly, and develop mildew.

MAINTAIN If the plant looks "tired" by midsummer, cut it back to 6 in (15 cm); water and feed it well, and it will produce fresh growth. If any all-green shoots appear, simply remove them. At the end of the summer this plant can be left in or taken out and then planted in the garden, in part shade.

HELIOTROPE *HELIOTROPIUM ARBORESCENS*

Loved by the Victorians, and popular with butterflies, too, this plant has flowers that vary from pale lilac to rich purple and smell of vanilla or cherry pie—just a few plants will perfume your patio. Although slow to get into their stride, by late summer they will be star performers in your display.

PLANT TYPE Half-hardy perennial; needs protection from frost and below 41°F (5°C) in winter

HEIGHT Up to 12 in (30 cm) in a pot, depending on varieties

SPREAD 12 in (30 cm) in a pot

POT SIZE Three plants per 12 in- (30 cm-) diameter pot, often combined with other plants

☼

CALENDAR

	WINTER	SPRING	SUMMER	FALL
IN LEAF		▨ ▨	▨ ▨	▨
IN FLOWER			▨ ▨	▨

COLOR

LEAVES Dark green, rough-textured, with a purple flush

FLOWERS Usually rich purple, but can be paler

The richly colored flowers of 'Marine' are most intense in a sunny spot.

CHOOSE

The most common kind of heliotrope is the striking, compact cultivar 'Marine', which has large, vibrant flower heads. 'Mini Marine' is similar, but smaller and more spreading. Both these plants are raised from seed.

Other attractive options include SCENTROPIA BLUE and SCENTROPIA SILVER, which are raised from cuttings, more spreading, and great for baskets. Older kinds, also raised from cuttings, include 'Chatsworth' with paler flowers but much stronger scent—this plant can reach 3 ft 3 in (1 m) in height.

PERFECT PARTNERS The dark foliage and flowers of heliotrope combine well with gray and silver foliage. **LARGE** *Laurus nobilis, Olea europaea, Trachelospermum jasminoides* **MEDIUM** *Lavandula, Nerium oleander* **SMALL** *Festuca glauca, Osteospermum, Verbena*

PLANT

You can sow heliotrope seeds in a propagator early in the spring. However, they are slow to grow at first and need warmth, good light, and careful watering. Seedlings should be grown on in cell trays until they are about 2 in (5 cm) high before putting them in containers to grow on.

Young plants must be protected from frost and grown, again in good light, until planting out in the late spring. Plants that are in flower during the summer months can be popped into containers at any time.

Grow heliotrope in a basket and you will not need to bend to sniff its flowers.

GROW

Heliotrope loves warmth and sunshine. Young plants will "sulk" if planted in large pots of wet potting mix, so make sure they are well grown in their nursery pots before planting them out. When mixing them with other plants in a large pot, ensure they do not get swamped by more vigorous plants. To boost growth, feed with liquid fertilizer when they begin to bloom.

MAINTAIN Each flower head blooms for many weeks. When most flowers have faded, cut off the whole head back to a leaf to encourage lower stems and more blooms. If the potting mix dries out too often they may suffer from mildew and aphid attack (see *pp.36–37*). At the end of the season, plants can be dug up, cut back, potted, and kept in frost-free conditions; growing from seed is easier.

TRAILING LOBELIA

LOBELIA ERINUS

Trailing lobelia, loved by bees and butterflies, cascades from baskets, window boxes, and planters, creating a waterfall of sparkling flowers. Shades of blue are popular but mixtures include pink, white, and red. Bushy lobelia are suitable for the edge of pots but look for the trailing types for baskets.

PLANT TYPE Half-hardy perennial grown as half-hardy annual; needs protection below 41°F (5°C)

HEIGHT 6in (15cm), in a pot, trailing to 12in (30cm)

SPREAD 6in (15cm)

POT SIZE Five plants per 12in- (30cm-) diameter pot; usually planted around the edge of other plants

☼ ☼

CALENDAR

	WINTER	SPRING	SUMMER	FALL
IN LEAF				
IN FLOWER				

COLOR

LEAVES Deep green or purple

FLOWERS Shades of blue, white, pink, or carmine-red

GROW

Once established, water regularly and give liquid fertilizer every week. Lobelias will flower freely at a young age, even when starved, but good feeding will encourage them to grow first and flower for longer. Water thoroughly when planted in baskets, where they are prone to drying out because they are positioned around the edge.

MAINTAIN If plants have stopped flowering and look straggly, trim them back to remove most of the stems and dead flowers. If watered and fed, they will sprout from the base and produce more flowers. If plants die, simply pull them out and let other plants fill in the gaps. Lobelia self-seed in cracks in paving the next year, so you may see some free plants the following season.

CHOOSE

Trailing lobelias are usually grown from seed, and the colors in the Cascade Series offer misty clouds of jewel-like flowers. These bloom very soon after planting. As they set seeds, the plants become scruffy, but it is not practical to deadhead so many tiny blooms.

New, cuttings-raised types that do not set seeds, such as the Waterfall Series, are more expensive but the blooms last and stay neat for far longer.

PERFECT PARTNERS Trailing lobelia is great mixed with other plants that have larger flowers; it is very useful in part shade. **LARGE** *Clematis, Nerium oleander, Salix integra* 'Hakuro-nishiki' **MEDIUM** *Dahlia, Hosta, Lavandula* **SMALL** *Begonia, Fuchsia, Nemesia*

PLANT

Buy young plants that are just coming into flower; avoid straggly plants that are in full flower as these may not grow much after planting. Keep your plants away from frost; if you are unable to protect them, delay buying them until the frosts have passed. They will flower less freely but live longer if they are planted in partial shade. Plant trailing lobelia around the edge of taller plants and around the edge of baskets.

Traditional, blue lobelia is a favorite to combine with red pelargoniums.

Be adventurous with mixed lobelia for a shower of dainty flowers in pastel tones.

GOLDEN CREEPING JENNY

LYSIMACHIA NUMMULARIA 'AUREA'

Golden creeping Jenny is a hardy, vigorous trailer that is grown for its bright yellow foliage. Although useful for containers, it is most often planted in wall pots and baskets to trail. It thrives in light shade as well as sun.

PLANT TYPE Hardy perennial; withstands frost

HEIGHT Up to 2 in (5 cm), trailing to up to 3 ft 3 in (1 m)

SPREAD 24 in (60 cm)

POT SIZE One plant per 12 in- (30 cm-) diameter pot; usually combined with other plants

☼ ☼

CALENDAR

	WINTER	SPRING	SUMMER	FALL
IN LEAF				
IN FLOWER			███	

COLOR

LEAVES Bright yellow, round leaves on trailing stems

FLOWERS Bright yellow

Golden creeping Jenny has striking yellow leaves as well as yellow blooms.

CHOOSE

Lysimachia nummularia is a vigorous plant that flowers freely, its yellow blooms offset by a mass of green leaves. Its cultivar 'Aurea', or golden creeping Jenny, is even more spectacular, with bright yellow flowers embraced by yellow leaves. It is a hardy plant that grows best in light shade and is ideal for hanging baskets and wall planters. Young plants can be planted at any time of the year.

Green-leaved *L. nummularia* lacks yellow leaves but has yellow blooms.

PERFECT PARTNERS Golden creeping Jenny is perfect for combining with orange or yellow begonias. It is a hardy plant, so it also partners well with spring flowers such as daffodils. **LARGE** *Acer palmatum, Fatsia japonica, Hedera* **MEDIUM** *Buxus sempervirens, Hosta* **SMALL** *Begonia, Fuchsia, Narcissus*

PLANT

Choose strong, young plants that are branched at the base. Pinch out the growing tips of any straggly shoots. Creeping Jenny prefers light shade and moist potting mix and will die if it is allowed to dry out. Good feeding and rich soil will promote vigorous growth, so mix time-release fertilizer with the potting mix.

If you want to grow this plant in hanging baskets, wall planters, or window boxes alongside other plants, be sure to position it around the edge of the container so that it can spill elegantly over the sides.

GROW

Keep plants well watered and fed at all times. Allow them to establish before hanging up baskets. Long trails can be trained around the edge of the potting mix to root, which will strengthen the plants and give a more bushy effect. Avoid very windy sites, which will damage the long trails of growth.

MAINTAIN Leaves turn brown if plants dry out. They will recover from short periods of drought, but it is best to cut away the affected stems. New shoots will appear, which will refresh the basket. At the beginning of fall, when baskets are emptied, cut back the plants or plant them in the garden or in other pots to grow next year.

PETUNIA *PETUNIA*

These colorful and often fragrant summer flowers are available in trailing and bushy types, with single or double flowers in an array of colors. Quick to grow and bloom, they are ideal for bringing color to sunny places. Those with white, pink, and purple flowers are especially fragrant.

PLANT TYPE Half-hardy perennial, usually grown as half-hardy annual; needs protection below 41°F (5°C)

HEIGHT 8 in (20 cm), or more, in a pot, some trailing to 30 in (75 cm)

SPREAD 8 in (20 cm), or more, in a pot

POT SIZE Three plants per 12 in- (30 cm-) diameter pot or large basket

☼ ☼

CALENDAR

	WINTER	SPRING	SUMMER	FALL
IN LEAF			▨▨	▨
IN FLOWER			▨▨▨	▨

COLOR

LEAVES Mid-green; a few have variegated leaves

FLOWERS Every color, from white to almost black, and in a range of interesting combinations

GROW

Petunias are easy to grow and reliable, although they dislike wet potting mix when they are small. Water carefully at first, until the plants are obviously established and growing strongly. Then water copiously and do not allow them to dry out. Pinching out growing tips when the plants are young can increase bushiness but is not essential.

When deadheading, remove the immature seed pod as well as the bloom.

MAINTAIN Most modern, cuttings-raised petunias do not set seed, so deadheading is purely aesthetic. But double flowers, in particular, can look scruffy as they age, so pull off the dead flowers regularly to help keep the plants looking good.

When deadheading other types of petunias, also nip off the seed pod—a messy job because of the sticky stems. Petunias respond well to regular feeding and, if well fed, will keep blooming for many months. Starved plants quickly show their age and should be replaced.

CHOOSE

Seed-raised petunias are the most economical option: they are often sold in packs, but need regular deadheading and do not have the color range of cuttings-raised types. These are sold in individual pots, often have intriguing colors, and include both double and trailing types, as in the Surfinia Series.

Petunias thrive in any sunny spot and are perfect for wall planters.

Always try to pick healthy, and not waterlogged, deep green plants. Most double-flowered kinds, such as Tumbelina Priscilla, have a compact but trailing habit, making them suitable for baskets, window boxes, and wall planters.

PERFECT PARTNERS Petunias are usually combined with other, tender, summer flowers but they can be planted with permanent plants to add extra color. **LARGE** *Canna, Ipomoea tricolor, Lathyrus odoratus* **MEDIUM** *Agapanthus, Penstemon, Yucca* **SMALL** *Begonia, Diascia, Verbena*

PLANT

These plants are easily damaged by frost, especially when young, so avoid planting them too early. When planting petunias, allow them room to grow as they vary greatly in vigor. Consider growing them on their own rather than with other plants as they can easily swamp smaller neighbors. Petunias are hungry plants, so mix time-release fertilizer into the potting mix before planting. They prefer to have a sunny place, out of strong wind.

TRAILING VERBENA *VERBENA*

With creeping stems and small leaves, verbenas are ideal mixers: their stems grow through other plants, which their dense heads of small flowers intermingle with. They bloom for months—the flowers are often sweetly scented and attract insects, especially butterflies and moths.

PLANT TYPE Half-hardy perennial, grown as half-hardy annual; needs protection below 41°F (5°C)

HEIGHT 8 in (20 cm), trailing to 12 in (30 cm)

SPREAD 8–12 in (20–30 cm)

POT SIZE Three plants per 12 in- (30 cm-) diameter pot; five plants per 16 in- (40 cm-) diameter pot

☼ ◐

CALENDAR

	WINTER	SPRING	SUMMER	FALL
IN LEAF		▨▨	▨▨	▨▨
IN FLOWER		▨▨	▨▨	▨▨

COLOR

LEAVES Deep green, often slightly hairy, toothed, or ferny

FLOWERS White, pink, red, mauve, or purple; often bicolored

Keep plants neat by removing flower clusters once the blooms have faded.

The small flowers are often scented and attract butterflies to the garden

CHOOSE

Trailing verbenas are available in many different shades. It is always worth sniffing them before buying, because several of them have a strong, sweet fragrance. The mixed-colored trailing verbenas sold in multipacks are usually grown from seed. These will be bushy in habit and need careful deadheading or they will set seed and stop blooming. The verbenas sold in individual pots will be grown from cuttings and superior in habit and flower power.

PERFECT PARTNERS Pastel verbenas combine well with silver and variegated plants, while brighter colors blend with vibrant bedding plants. **LARGE** *Melianthus major, Nerium oleander, Salix integra* 'Hakuro-nishiki' **MEDIUM** *Dahlia, Pelargonium* **SMALL** *Festuca glauca, Heliotropium arborescens, Lobelia erinus*

PLANT

Young verbena plants are highly sensitive to overwatering, so make sure they are well rooted when you buy them. If you buy them before the last frost of spring, protect them from cold—verbenas will survive a light frost when mature, but not as tender young plants. Pinch out the growing tips when planting to encourage bushiness and more flowers later.

GROW

Once in growth, water regularly. Do not allow the plants to dry out or they will be prone to mildew. One month after planting, feed once a week with liquid fertilizer. Pinch off flower clusters when the last flowers have dropped. Peg down shoots (with small, bent wires or a stone) across the potting mix surface to encourage rooting, which will improve plant vigor.

MAINTAIN If your plants are attacked by aphids, rub the affected leaves between your fingers. In late summer, when the plants get scruffy, rejuvenate them by trimming them back and increasing their feed to stimulate new growth. Plants, or freshly rooted cuttings, can be saved for another year if cut back and kept in a bright, frost-free place (although young plants are readily available in spring).

Flowers are fleeting but foliage is forever. Be sure to include some plants with interesting and colorful foliage, such as heucheras, in your garden or patio so that you always have a vibrant display, even without flowers.

FOR FOLIAGE

As well as being beautiful for months, leaves can be as colorful and varied as flowers. Make them the basis of your planting plans and you're well on the way to creating a stunning outdoor display, packed with drama and interest.

VIBRANT COLOR

Leaves are not just green—many plants have variegated forms that add variety to plant groups. The greatest variations are found among hostas, which are at their brightest in their variegated kinds, splashed and streaked with yellow and white. Heucheras show an even greater range of colors to suit every taste and, being more or less evergreen, are beautiful all year, allowing some vibrant combinations with flowers. Both plants also flower, and though their blooms are not the main appeal, they are loved by bees and bring life to your patio in summer.

DRAMATIC SHAPES

If you want drama, look to leaves. The Abyssinian banana has the biggest leaves you can grow in a garden and though it will need protection from cold in winter is well worth the effort for its huge, paddle-shaped leaves that flap in the breeze in summer. Melianthus is hardier, but the gray, lush leaves are just as striking, making a bold contrast to virtually every

other plant in the garden. New Zealand flax (*Phormium*) is also eye-catching, with long, arching, evergreen leaves. These magnificent plants are immensely popular for containers and come in a wide range of sizes and colors, from near-black to stripes of red, pink, and yellow.

SEASONAL VARIATION

Most plants are more lush and have greener leaves in summer, though spring sometimes brings a colorful flush to new foliage. Heucheras will be brightest as their fresh leaves emerge and the autumn fern (*Dryopteris erythrosora*) is also colorful as new fronds appear, often in spring but also in summer. The ever-changing tapestry of its hues brings interest to any shady place. Evergreen grasses, including the spiky blue fescue (*Festuca glauca*), keep their looks all year, but deciduous grasses change with the seasons. Japanese forest grass (*Hakonechloa macra*), a beautiful grass for pots, is fresh as a daisy in spring, reveals an elegant, arching habit in summer, and is a celebration of all the colors of fall as the year draws to a close.

TREE HOUSELEEK

AEONIUM ARBOREUM

These tough, drought-resistant plants with tall stems and rosettes of fleshy leaves will tolerate infrequent watering. They vary in size and color, but all are dramatic options for summer gardens, acting as a striking contrast to more familiar plants, and are easy to care for.

PLANT TYPE Tender, succulent shrub; needs protection from frost and temperatures below 41°F (5°C)
HEIGHT Up to 24in (60cm) in a pot
SPREAD Up to 18in (45cm) in a pot
POT SIZE One plant per 8in- (20cm-) diameter pot

CALENDAR

	WINTER		SPRING		SUMMER		FALL	
IN LEAF								
IN FLOWER								

COLOR

LEAVES Green, variegated with white or very dark purple
FLOWERS Yellow

Green aeoniums grow quicker than the black plants, and often have yellow flowers.

CHOOSE

The architectural shape and fleshy rosettes of tree houseleek are striking in any setting. The cultivar 'Zwartkop' is a classic choice, with its dark purple leaves around a green center. There are many similar options, including 'Poldark' and 'Merry Maiden'. Other plants have variegated leaves, such as 'Sunburst', or a more compact, branching habit. All need a sunny spot.

PERFECT PARTNERS Tree houseleek combines particularly well with other sun-loving plants that have bold and eye-catching foliage. **LARGE** *Cordyline australis, Olea europaea, Trachelospermum jasminoides* **MEDIUM** *Agapanthus, Correa pulchella, Dahlia* **SMALL** *Pelargonium, Sempervivum tectorum*

PLANT

Buy young plants in spring or summer and pot into slightly larger pots. Use a well-drained, cactus potting mix or commercial potting mix with some added grit or perlite. Plants are often top-heavy and difficult to keep upright when they are first planted, so they may need to be supported by canes until they are rooted. For greater impact, plant three small tree houseleeks together in the same pot.

Black-leaved aeoniums develop the best color in full sun and when quite dry.

GROW

Do not overwater these succulents. They grow best in stone or terra-cotta pots that dry out quickly. Too much water and fertilizer in summer can encourage large leaves and rosettes and soft stems that cannot support the growth. Large rosettes produce conical clusters of yellow flowers in late spring.

MAINTAIN If growth becomes leggy, cut off large rosettes with a length of stem, 2in (5cm) or more. Allow them to dry out for a day, then root them in pots of gritty potting mix. New shoots grow from the cut stem to make a bushy plant. Bring inside before the first frost of fall. Frost will kill the top growth, although the lower stem may survive. Tree houseleeks are prone to attack by vine weevils (see *p.36*).

AUTUMN FERN

DRYOPTERIS ERYTHROSORA

This hardy plant thrives in shade and combines the feathery elegance of fern fronds with startling orange and bronze tones. Young plants show their bright colors as they grow and can be used in mixed pots, while more mature specimens deserve a pot to themselves.

PLANT TYPE Hardy, evergreen perennial
HEIGHT Up to 24 in (60 cm) in a pot
SPREAD Up to 18 in (45 cm) in a pot
POT SIZE One plant per 12 in- (30 cm-) diameter pot; three plants per 16 in- (40 cm-) diameter pot

☼ ☀

CALENDAR

	WINTER	SPRING	SUMMER	FALL
IN LEAF	░	░	░	░
IN FLOWER				

COLOR

LEAVES Bright orange or rust when young, maturing to dark green
FLOWERS None

Keep ferns healthy, like this *D. filix-mas*, by checking for vine-weevil grubs.

Autumn fern is most colorful in spring, but the fronds are showy all year.

CHOOSE

The graceful yet hardy autumn ferns are among the easiest of all the ferns to care for. There are a number of cultivars that have slight differences in the intensity of the young foliage, including 'Brilliance' and 'Radiance'.

However, if you are in search of a larger, more robust species, try *D. filix-mas*, with green, upright foliage.

Alternatively, *D. cycadina*, has coarser foliage, gives a tropical effect, and is often evergreen in sheltered areas.

PERFECT PARTNERS Ferns have a natural affinity with evergreen shrubs and with other plants that have elegant foliage. **LARGE** *Acer palmatum, Phyllostachys, Pseudopanax lessonii* **MEDIUM** *Helleborus, Lilium, Narcissus* **SMALL** *Hakonechloa macra, Hosta, Lysimachia nummularia* 'Aurea'

PLANT

Buy plants in spring or summer when they are in full growth and have young leaves. Plant them in their own pots or with other plants with similar needs—shade and moist potting mix. An organically enriched mix is best, but standard mixes suit their need for moisture. Mix in some time-release fertilizer before planting. Small plants can be added under large specimen shrubs to give interest at ground level.

GROW

The key to healthy ferns is to keep them moist at all times. Autumn ferns are among the toughest and best for pots, but they must never be neglected. In hot, dry spells, move their pots under taller plants to prevent scorching.

MAINTAIN Although usually evergreen, it may need a tidy up in spring to remove old leaves, which will also help present the colorful new growth better. You can safely remove a few fronds to shape the plant, too, if it is grown in a pot with other plants. If plants lose vigor, divide and replant them in spring. Autumn fern's main enemy is vine weevil grubs (see p.36), so check plants if you suspect you have these pests in the garden.

ABYSSINIAN BANANA

ENSETE VENTRICOSUM

This majestic plant will become the focal point of your displays. Its huge leaves create a lush, jungle effect and welcome shade on a sheltered patio. Perfect for impatient gardeners, it grows rapidly if well watered and even a young plant will make an impact by the end of the first summer.

PLANT TYPE Tender, evergreen perennial; needs protection from wind and from temperatures below 32°F (0°C)

HEIGHT Up to 7 ft 9 in (2.4 m) in a pot

SPREAD Up to 7 ft 9 in (2.4 m) in a pot

POT SIZE One plant per 12 in- (30 cm-) diameter pot; needs a larger pot within a year

☼ ◐

CALENDAR

	WINTER		SPRING		SUMMER		FALL	
IN LEAF	░	░	░	░	░	░	░	░
IN FLOWER								

COLOR

LEAVES Bright green often with red midribs; suffused with dark red in the cultivar 'Maurelii'

FLOWERS Unlikely in a pot

Green-leaved Abyssinian bananas grow rapidly if well fed and watered.

CHOOSE

This dramatic plant, with its large, bright green, oblong leaves, is the most widely grown *Ensete*. But many choose the cultivar 'Maurelii' for its deep red stalks and reddish leaves, which color best in full sun. Both are wider and have larger leaves than the hardy banana (see p.46). A smaller but similar plant to *E. ventricosum* is *Musa lasiocarpa*, which has spreading, gray-green leaves.

PERFECT PARTNERS Make the most of this exuberant beauty with other lush foliage and vibrant flowers. **LARGE** *Canna, Miscanthus sinensis, Phyllostachys* **MEDIUM** *Melianthus major, Hemerocallis, Phormium* **SMALL** *Begonia, Dahlia, Pelargonium*

PLANT

This plant is not frost tolerant, so delay planting until early summer. It grows rapidly and will need a roomy pot. Any good potting mix is suitable, but add some time-release fertilizer to it because this is a hungry plant.

Abyssinian banana should last for many years, so either give it a pot to itself or surround it with summer bedding plants that can be removed from the pot at the end of the summer, when it must be brought under cover.

'Maurelii' is popular for the intense dark red coloration of its leaf stalks.

GROW

How big and fast your Abyssinian banana grows will depend on how much you water and feed it. A small plant can easily reach 6 ft 6 in (2 m) in just a single season, if kept moist and fed every week, but you can keep it smaller on a leaner diet. Grow in a sheltered site to prevent the leaves from being torn by wind.

MAINTAIN Cut off scruffy leaves as they age, leaving the base of the leaf stalk. Remove most of the foliage, leaving just the central, upright leaves. Move to a cool, frost-free place for winter. Keep the plant just moist, without letting it dry out. It can also be kept in a cool, bright spot in the home during winter.

EUPHORBIA *EUPHORBIA CHARACIAS*

This Mediterranean shrub boasts elegant gray-green leaves, like bottlebrushes, on upright stems all year. The stems are topped with lime-green flowers in spring. It thrives in sunny spots, and the feathery texture and spectacular blooms mix well with other evergreens as well as with spring bulbs.

PLANT TYPE Hardy, evergreen shrub; may be damaged by prolonged extreme cold
HEIGHT Up to 3 ft 3 in (1 m) in a pot
SPREAD Up to 3 ft 3 in (1 m) in a pot
POT SIZE One plant per 12 in- (30 cm-) diameter pot; needs a larger pot as it grows
☼

CALENDAR

	WINTER	SPRING	SUMMER	FALL
IN LEAF	▓	▓	▓	▓
IN FLOWER		▓		

COLOR

LEAVES Gray-green, sometimes tinged purple in winter
FLOWERS Lime green to yellow

Some *E. characias* have striking black "eyes" instead of the more common gold.

Variegated euphorbias are ideal for pots and remain vigorous all year.

CHOOSE

The species *Euphorbia characias* has two subspecies: subsp. *characias*, with showy bracts that have dark "eyes," and subsp. *wulfenii*, with yellow centers. The stunning, variegated cultivar *E. characias* 'Tasmanian Tiger' has cream-edged leaves and is about half the size of the plain green euphorbia. If you have a shady site, try the smaller *E.* × *martini*, which has dark green leaves and lime-green flowers, or *E. amygdaloides* 'Purpurea', with purple leaves and lime-green flowers.

PERFECT PARTNERS Euphorbia's gray-green leaves and Mediterranean origin suit terra-cotta containers that are planted with other gray plants and grasses. **LARGE** *Cordyline australis*, *Ficus carica*, *Olea europaea* **MEDIUM** *Chamaerops humilis*, *Dahlia*, *Yucca* **SMALL** *Nerine bowdenii*

PLANT

Euphorbia needs an enriched potting mix. Each stem lives for two years. In the first year, it grows to its maximum height, and in the next spring, the top unfurls to produce blooms. The stem then dies. If you buy a plant in spring, when the blooms fade to brown, cut down the stem to where you can see new shoots appearing. These new shoots will flower the following year.

GROW

This plant is drought-tolerant once established but will grow better if it is kept moist throughout the summer. Feed once a week during spring and summer because strong growth then will produce the best blooms the following spring. Turn the plant, if possible, to produce even growth, especially if it is positioned against a wall. If the plant is in an exposed spot, protect it from winter gales, which could snap off its stems.

MAINTAIN As the flowers fade they can be attacked by aphids (see p.36). To prevent this and to keep the plant tidy, remove the flowered stems as they age. The sap of euphorbias is toxic and an irritant, so wear gloves when pruning and avoid the sap getting in contact with broken skin or the eyes or mouth.

BLUE FESCUE *FESTUCA GLAUCA*

This is the most popular ornamental grass, loved for its tactile qualities and the color of its needlelike leaves. Blue fescue looks good in its own pot or mixed with a wide variety of plants. You can divide established clumps and experiment with planting ideas all over your sunny patio.

PLANT TYPE Hardy, evergreen, perennial grass
HEIGHT Up to 8 in (20 cm) in a pot
SPREAD Up to 8 in (20 cm) in a pot
POT SIZE Three plants per 12 in- (30 cm-) diameter pot

CALENDAR

	WINTER	SPRING	SUMMER	FALL
IN LEAF				
IN FLOWER				

COLOR

LEAVES Steely blue or gray
FLOWERS Steely blue or gray

Hanging pots suit blue fescue (bottom), which does not mix well with some plants.

CHOOSE

The many cultivars of the steely blue ornamental grass *Festuca glauca* have subtle variations: for example, 'Elijah Blue' is compact, while INTENSE BLUE is larger than most and somewhat shaggy. 'Blaufuchs' probably comes closest to a true blue, whereas 'Golden Toupee' is a complete contrast, with leaves that start out as bright yellow in spring, but later turn to a grayish green.

The blue-green foliage of *F. glauca* INTENSE BLUE is attractive all year.

An alternative to *F. glauca* is another evergreen, *Helictotrichon sempervirens*, which is also blue, but looser in habit and taller, reaching 3 ft 3 in (1 m) high.

PERFECT PARTNERS The crisp color of blue fescue combines well with pinks and grays, and it also suits other sun-loving plants. **LARGE** *Juniperus scopulorum* 'Skyrocket', *Olea europaea*, *Salix integra* 'Hakuro-nishiki' **MEDIUM** *Euphorbia characias*, *Melianthus major*, *Penstemon* **SMALL** *Dianthus*, *Diascia*, *Lavandula*

PLANT

Blue fescue can be planted at any time of the year, but the grasses prefer to be planted and divided in springtime. They are often grown in commercial potting mix, but this tends to dry out rapidly so make sure you soak the roots before planting to keep them moist.

This is a plant that dislikes boisterous neighbors that will shade it or smother it, causing it to rot. Do not plant blue fescue too deep in the potting mix or it can rot. A gritty potting mix is best so that it is not too wet in the winter.

GROW

Keep evenly moist and feed once a week during the growing season. Slim flower stalks appear in summer but these are unattractive and best sheared off before they turn brown, soon after the flowers are produced. Do not let leaves or flowers from taller plants remain on the foliage or rot can develop.

MAINTAIN Apart from removing flower stems, you will not need to do much until spring, when the plant can be sheared off at about 3 in (8 cm) high. This will remove the old, brown leaves and show off the new, spring growth. After two or three years, plants can become dead in the center of the clump. If this happens, dig up and pull the plant into sections in spring, replant them, discarding the dead, central area.

FIG *FICUS CARICA*

The leaves of the fig are among the most striking of all hardy trees. Although potentially large trees, figs grow well in pots and are more likely to produce fruit when their roots are restricted. Regular pruning results in large, spectacular leaves, perfect for any subtropical planting plan.

PLANT TYPE Hardy, deciduous tree; tolerates frost
HEIGHT Up to 7 ft 9 in (2.4 m) in a pot
SPREAD Up to 6 ft 6 in (2 m) in a pot
POT SIZE One plant per 12 in- (30 cm-) diameter pot; needs a larger pot after a year

CALENDAR

	WINTER	SPRING	SUMMER	FALL
IN LEAF		▓▓	▓▓▓▓	▓▓
IN FLOWER				

COLOR

LEAVES Rough-textured and dark green; may turn yellow in fall before dropping
FLOWERS Insignificant

GROW

Keep the plant moist and feed once a week with fertilizer. Figs tend to become leggy as they grow, but they can be pruned in spring or at any time in summer. Remove the growing tips of the shoots in midsummer. This will promote side shoots that carry tiny figs over winter—the fruit will ripen the following summer.

MAINTAIN To produce the most dramatic foliage, at the expense of fruit, hard prune the stems in spring. This will give vigorous stems with large leaves. In fall, the leaves will turn yellow and drop.

If you want fruit, it may be necessary to protect the figlets on the branches by covering with fleece in cold spells or moving the plant into a greenhouse; but this is not essential if you are not hoping for fruit. Any stems damaged by cold can be pruned back in spring.

Figs are easily trained as effective standards with single, bare stems.

CHOOSE

The fig plant most widely available in garden centers is *Ficus carica* 'Brown Turkey', which is a hardy plant that is likely to produce fruit in a sunny, warm spot. The impressive, large, lobed leaves of 'Brown Turkey' are the classic shape of the familiar fig leaf. Other good cultivars to watch out for include 'Ice Crystal', with deeply lobed, filigree leaves that resemble snowflakes, and 'Panachée', with plain green leaves and fruit and stems that have distinctive yellow and green stripes.

PERFECT PARTNERS Combine a fig with large-leaved foliage plants or vibrant summer flowers for a feel of the tropics. **LARGE** *Canna, Musa basjoo* **MEDIUM** *Choisya, Melianthus major, Phormium* **SMALL** *Dahlia, Osteospermum, Pelargonium*

PLANT

Figs are usually potted in enriched potting mix and kept underpotted to restrict growth and encourage fruit production: if grown for their foliage, this is not essential. But pot your new plant into a container that is a bit bigger than the one you bought it in. Then, after a year, move it into a larger pot. Figs are drought-tolerant but will grow better if well fed and watered. They can get tall, so use weighty pots for stability.

Prune figs in spring, removing long, straggly stems to keep a neat shape.

JAPANESE FOREST GRASS *HAKONECHLOA MACRA*

PLANT TYPE Hardy perennial
HEIGHT Up to 12 in (30 cm) in a pot
SPREAD Up to 18 in (45 cm) in a pot
POT SIZE One plant per 12 in- (30 cm-) diameter pot; three plants per 16 in- (40 cm-) diameter pot

☼ ☼

Neat and compact, this grass makes domed mopheads when mature, with elegantly arching, narrow leaves. It contrasts with bolder foliage and benefits from a tall pot so that its elegant habit can be fully appreciated.

CALENDAR

	WINTER	SPRING	SUMMER	FALL
IN LEAF				
IN FLOWER				

COLOR

LEAVES Mid-green or striped with yellow or all yellow, according to cultivar
FLOWERS Green

GROW

Water to keep the potting mix moist and feed once a week to encourage strong growth. Because it is grown for foliage, a general plant food is preferable to a flowering plant food. If plants dry out or are in a very hot spot, the foliage may scorch or bleach. They have a less upright habit in shade. Protect young growth in spring from snails and slugs.

MAINTAIN Plants need little extra care during the summer, but when the foliage turns brown in fall it can be trimmed back—leave this task until spring, if you prefer, but it should certainly be trimmed off before any new growth appears in spring. Old or crowded plants can be divided into sections in spring and repotted.

CHOOSE

This graceful plant has green or yellow leaves that deepen to russet tones in fall, when they are enhanced by delicate, wispy flower stems.

The cultivar 'Aureola', which has leaves striped with green and yellow, is very popular. 'Alboaurea' has brighter, variegated leaves and 'All Gold' has plain yellow leaves. All have the same habit.

For more shady areas, try *Milium effusum* 'Aureum', a golden grass with a sparse habit that grows through other plants and often self-seeds.

PERFECT PARTNERS This grass contrasts with red and orange flowers and bold, rounded leaves and upright plants. **LARGE** *Acer palmatum*, *Fatsia japonica*, *Hedera* **MEDIUM** *Buxus sempervirens*, *Lilium*, *Sarcococca* **SMALL** *Dryopteris erythrosora*, *Heuchera*, *Hosta*

PLANT

Young plants can be potted at any time of year, ideally into enriched potting mix. They are usually one-sided when young and do not reveal their mature habit until a few years old. They can be planted under large shrubs in big pots and also in window boxes and hanging baskets, where they will grow toward the light and cascade from the edge. Underplant this grass with permanent bulbs such as daffodils or short tulips.

Tousled heads of variegated leaves bring movement and color to patio pots.

Trim back the leaves in fall, when they change to more russet tones.

HEUCHERA *HEUCHERA*

Heucheras, along with their related hybrids, are the most colorful of evergreen foliage plants. Their leaves come in a bewildering array of colors and are especially bright in spring, when new leaves appear. Airy sprays of small flowers add extra interest and are loved by bees.

PLANT TYPE Hardy perennial with evergreen foliage

HEIGHT Leaves up to 10 in (25 cm); flowers up to 18 in (45 cm) in a pot

SPREAD Up to 10 in (25 cm) in a pot

POT SIZE One plant per 8 in- (20 cm-) diameter pot; three plants per 12 in- (30 cm-) pot

☼ ◑

CALENDAR

	WINTER	SPRING	SUMMER	FALL
IN LEAF				
IN FLOWER				

COLOR

LEAVES According to variety, matt or glossy and green, almost black, purple, orange, red, or yellow

FLOWERS Most are small and white but can be pink, red, yellow, or orange

Dark-leaved heucheras are a vibrant contrast to bright green foliage plants.

'Sweet Tea' is a vigorous plant that has dainty summer flowers and color all year.

CHOOSE

Dark-leaved heucheras, such as the cultivar 'Obsidian', offset silver and gray leaves and look best in sun. Bright 'Lime Marmalade' and vibrant 'Lime Rickey' will shimmer in shady areas. 'Fire Alarm' and 'Cherry Cola' have fiery yellow and orange flowers. Intergeneric hybrids × *heucherella* 'Sweet Tea' and 'Brass Lantern' have a more spreading habit and are best in shade.

PERFECT PARTNERS Heucheras mix well with vibrant flowers and leaves in summer and winter. **LARGE** *Acer palmatum, Salix integra* 'Hakuro-nishiki', *Hydrangea anomala* subsp. *petiolaris* **MEDIUM** *Astelia chathamica, Buxus sempervirens, Phormium* **SMALL** *Euonymus fortunei, Hakonechloa macra, Helleborus*

PLANT

Heucheras can be planted at any time of the year, although they are ideal for summer and winter containers, so they are most often planted in spring or fall. They like a rich and open, but not a wet potting mix. Either use a mix intended for cactus, or add grit or perlite to potting mix.

Plant your heucheras at the same level as in their original pot, and not too deeply. They grow well with other plants, so they can be mixed with flowers and foliage of all types in one pot. Plant bulbs around them for spring displays.

GROW

Heucheras will be more compact and flower more freely in a sunny place. Keep them moist and feed weekly in summer to promote healthy foliage. When flowers fade, trim back the old stems. New foliage in spring covers the old leaves and looks good all summer. Trim off some of the old, outer foliage in fall and spring to tidy the plants.

MAINTAIN Vine-weevil grubs are the plant's main enemy (see p.36): they eat the roots, causing the plant to stop growing and fall out of its pot. After several years, heucheras can become unsightly, with bare stems. In fall or spring, dig them up, split them into sections, and replant them with the "trunk" buried.

HOSTA *HOSTA*

These hardy perennials, grown mainly for their foliage, are deciduous and die back in fall, with fresh leaves emerging in spring. With hundreds of cultivars available, there is immense variation in size and leaf color. Many hostas are ideal for sun or part shade in almost any garden.

PLANT TYPE Hardy perennial

HEIGHT 4 in–3 ft 3 in (10 cm–1 m), or more, in a pot

SPREAD 6–36 in (15–90 cm), or more, in a pot

POT SIZE One to three plants per 12 in- (30 cm-) diameter pot, according to size of cultivar

☼ ☼

CALENDAR

	WINTER	SPRING	SUMMER	FALL
IN LEAF				
IN FLOWER				

COLOR

LEAVES Yellow, green, blue-gray, or variegated

FLOWERS White, lilac, mauve, or purple

PERFECT PARTNERS Because of their wide variations in size and leaf color, hostas combine well with a range of plants. Their bold, rounded leaf-shape offsets grassy and narrow foliage and delicate ferns. **LARGE** *Acer palmatum*, *Canna*, *Hedera* **MEDIUM** *Dryopteris*, *Hakonechloa*, *Hemerocallis* **SMALL** *Helleborus*, *Heuchera*, *Narcissus*

CHOOSE

Hostas vary in appearance, and requirements, though all need a moist potting mix and a bright spot away from intense sun. They have a great range of leaf colors, but make sure you choose one that suits your situation:

hostas with yellow leaves need some sun to develop their full color, while the blue-gray cultivars need part shade. In sun, they lose their waxy leaf coating and scorch. Most variegated hostas are best with sun for half the day.

Plants come in a vast range of sizes, so they can be used in small, shallow pans and window boxes, or as large specimens in pots; they can also be happily included in mixed plantings in pots. Among the biggest hostas are 'Empress Wu', which will reach 3 ft 3 in (1 m), or more, in a pot (far more in the ground), and 'Guacamole', 'Fried Green Tomatoes', and 'Sum and Substance', which have fragrant flowers.

Among the smallest hostas are the popular 'Blue Mouse Ears' and the tiny, variegated 'Pandora's Box', just 4 in (10 cm) high. In between these, there are hundreds of hostas to choose from. 'Praying Hands' and its variegated sport 'Hands Up' are distinctive for their upright leaves, and 'Krossa Regal' has an upright, arching shape. Narrow-leaved 'Ginko Craig' and 'Tattle Tails' soon form spreading clumps—ideal for underplanting deciduous shrubs.

'Hands Up' is a striking and unusual foliage plant that thrives in a pot.

Large-leaved hostas bring lushness and interest to pots in the shade.

PLANT

Hostas can be planted at any time of the year, but spring and summer are best for immediate impact. Plant them in enriched potting mix. As with all plants, water them well before planting and soak well after planting to settle the roots in the potting mix.

If you are planting in spring, and if the pot contains a large clump with many shoots, this clump can be carefully divided. To do this, shake off the excess soil and cut the clump into two or more parts, making sure each part has at least one shoot. The divided plants need extra care while they establish.

It is preferable to place your pots in part shade initially, while they establish, before experimenting with moving them into brighter positions.

When hostas produce shoots in spring, cut through the woody base and pull sections apart, then replant them in fresh potting mix.

GROW

Hostas must always be kept moist to maintain healthy foliage. The leaves that unfurl in spring will remain all summer, often with a second flush in the middle of summer, along with flowers. Either feed them every week with a general fertilizer or apply a season-long fertilizer in spring to maintain growth. Flowers are produced in summer. To keep plants tidy, remove the faded flower spikes by cutting them off at the base.

Blue-leaved hostas scorch in full sun. If this happens, move them to a shady spot. Debris—fallen leaves and flowers from overhead shrubs—can gather on their leaves and cause discoloration.

Slugs and snails eat hosta leaves and the damage is obvious for months. It is important to protect your plants from them as soon as the shoots appear in spring. Good hygiene, removing fallen leaves around pots in spring, checking for snails around the rim or pots, and looking for slugs under pots—all will help minimize damage. Covering the potting mix with coarse grit and broken eggshells is also a deterrent (see p.37).

Snails enjoy feasting on hosta leaves, especially in wet weather.

MAINTAIN Hostas are long-lived perennials and can remain in their pots for many years. In fall, when the leaves turn yellow and die down, cut them off, along with any remaining flower stems, to remove hiding places for snails. Leave the pots outside in winter and water if the pots are in the rain shadow of the house and likely to dry out. Your plants will eventually become crowded in the pots; when this happens, repot them into a larger pot or divide them and replant some of the sections in the original pot. This is best done in spring, just as the new growth appears.

Most hostas do not reach their full potential for years. Leaf and plant size and variegation may not show their typical patterning until mature. Dividing plants can affect this, and they may not grow as large as usual immediately after dividing clumps; but simple repotting will not affect this, and should increase the leaf size of plants that have been dwarfed by being pot-bound previously.

Fall brings changes to hostas—cut off the yellow and dying leaves.

HONEY FLOWER

MELIANTHUS MAJOR

This architectural, evergreen shrub steals the show with its handsome, boldly divided, silvery foliage. It can be grown as a low, bushy plant or a tall shrub, depending on pruning and winter protection. If grown tall, it presents spires of dark red flowers that produce abundant nectar—hence its name.

PLANT TYPE Tender shrub; needs protection below 32°F (0°C); can survive short periods of frost.

HEIGHT Up to 6 ft 6 in (2 m) in a pot

SPREAD Up to 3 ft 3 in (1 m) in a pot

POT SIZE One plant per 12 in- (30 cm-) diameter pot; needs a larger pot after a few years

CALENDAR

	WINTER	SPRING	SUMMER	FALL
IN LEAF				
IN FLOWER				

COLOR

LEAVES Steely gray; may lose leaves in winter

FLOWERS Beet-red

GROW

The plant's growth depends on feeding and watering. Keep potting mix moist and feed every week to encourage strong stems and large leaves. It will be more lush if in a sunny, warm, sheltered spot. If too dark, the stems may become weak and need staking. When growing well, new shoots will appear from the base to create a thick, lush plant.

MAINTAIN The plant becomes more scruffy in winter. Severe cold kills the stems, so protect the crown with a covering of straw, secured by chicken wire, or move the pot to a greenhouse. In spring, if stems have died, trim them off just above the soil and new stems will appear when the weather warms.

CHOOSE

This is the most common species of *Melianthus* available and, with its large and dramatic saw-toothed leaves, is the best species for a striking foliage effect. The plant's dark red flowers are a secondary feature and are produced on stems that have survived winter into their second season.

You will only see honey flowers if you live in an extremely mild area or have protected the plant from frost. But the magnificent, lush foliage is the main attraction—so even if your plant is cut down by severe frost, it is still well worth growing.

PERFECT PARTNERS The honey flower combines well with other lush foliage plants and contrasting, strap-like leaves. **LARGE** *Canna, Fatsia japonica, Musa basjoo* **MEDIUM** *Euphorbia, Hemerocallis, Phormium* **SMALL** *Carex, Pelargonium*

PLANT

This is a strong-growing, large plant that will remain in its pot for several years. Plant in enriched potting mix with seasonal bedding plants around the edge, but take care, as it can swamp small plants in the same container if it grows vigorously. Plant your honey flower in late spring so that it will be fully established before winter.

The metallic effect of honey flower's leaves add interest to any garden.

Light frosts will stop honey flower's growth but will rarely damage its leaves.

NEW ZEALAND FLAX

PHORMIUM

New Zealand flax offer a wide variety of looks, from tidy clumps of colorful leaves to large, arching plants that will dominate any plant group. They are evergreen and survive in windy and coastal gardens, but they dislike extreme cold. Although they flower, it is the foliage that steals the show.

PLANT TYPE Evergreen perennial; frost hardy but may need protection in extreme cold weather

HEIGHT 18 in–7 ft 9 in (45 cm–2.4 m), according to type

SPREAD 24 in–7 ft 9 in (60 cm– 2.4 m), according to type

POT SIZE One plant per 12 in- (30 cm-) diameter pot

☼ ☀

CALENDAR

	WINTER	SPRING	SUMMER	FALL
IN LEAF				
IN FLOWER				

COLOR

LEAVES Green, purple, red, pink, yellow, or cream

FLOWERS Dark red

GROW

Keep your New Zealand flax plants moist and in full sun. When grown in shade, the leaves will lose their original color and may become floppy. Pull off or cut off old leaves that turn brown as they age. Healthy plants produce tall stems of tubular, dark red flowers that can be ugly when they fade and need cutting off at the base.

MAINTAIN In spring, remove any leaves that are tattered or in poor condition. Resist the temptation to cut through them as the cut ends will turn brown and look ugly. Remove the leaves completely if the plants get too big for your liking. Wind can thrash these swordlike leaves around, which can cause great damage to nearby plants.

Tall containers enhance the arching leaves of dwarf New Zealand flax.

CHOOSE

New Zealand flax, has striking, strap-like leaves that come in various colors and stripes. There are two species: *Phormium colensoi* is small with arching leaves, while *P. tenax* is considerably taller and more upright with towering flower spikes.

These two species have produced many hybrids with colorful leaves, including: 'Bronze Baby', with dark brown leaves; 'Yellow Wave' and 'Duet', with leaves that are striped in yellow; and 'Pink Panther' and 'Flamingo', with leaves striped in pink.

PERFECT PARTNERS The architectural leaves look great with other bold leaves; the colors suit many planting plans. **LARGE** *Ensete ventricosum, Fatsia japonica, Hedera* **MEDIUM** *Chamaerops humilis, Melianthus major, Pseudopanax lessonii* **SMALL** *Alstroemeria, Correa pulchella*

PLANT

These tough plants withstand drought but their roots are vulnerable to frost when grown in containers, so it is best to line the pot with bubble wrap before adding potting mix.

Plant in spring or summer so plants can get established before winter. Use enriched potting mix and time-release fertilizer. Plant at the same level as in the original pot, but never deeper. Water well after planting to settle.

Avoid trimming these plants across their leaves as it will disfigure them.

Every garden needs a few plants that can be relied on to bloom for as long as possible, providing great clouds of blossoms and color, like these glorious argyranthemums and nemesias.

FOR COLOR

Color is a powerful element in any garden or patio and can be used in numerous ways: to create high drama or bold statements, for example, or in more gentle, harmonious plans, and even to add a simple accent here and there.

BEAUTIFUL BULBS

If you want to pack color into your garden or patio, choose bulbs. They will take up very little space and can be planted under other plants, blooming above and between them. Lilies offer an enormous range of colors and shapes and many of them are heavily fragrant, making your patio a heavenly place to be during the summer months. For magnificent spring color, plant daffodils: choose dwarf kinds for small pots and window boxes and taller kinds for large containers, growing up through spring flowers and among perennials. Easy to care for and giving great value, they can be left in their pots for many years and will increase in beauty every spring.

NO-NONSENSE PERENNIALS

Most gardeners fill patio containers with flowers for summer, replacing them each spring. But long-lived perennials are also a terrific option that will pack in plenty of flowers and foliage and come back, stronger, year after year. Among these,

alstroemerias are essential for a sunny patio. Available in a variety of heights and colors, they provide a nonstop display of color from early summer to late fall and are trouble-free and easy to grow. Daylilies have bold, arching leaves and their beautiful flowers will bring a touch of glamour to your garden or patio. Known for their reliability and ease of growth, they, too, get bigger and better as the years go by.

TENDER BLOOMS

Grow some tender plants with eye-catching colors for many months of blooms—once they start to flower, they continue right until the frosts of fall. Most can be saved for another year if protected from cold in winter, but even when treated as disposable they are great value because of their long flowering season. These are some of the most popular plants of all and include familiar favorites, such as French marigolds and dahlias, along with more recent introductions, including nemesias and diascias, which have become increasingly popular because they bloom for so many months.

PERUVIAN LILY *ALSTROEMERIA*

Forming dense cushions of lush foliage, and covered in long-lasting flowers, Peruvian lilies are perfect for containers in any sunny spot. Their range of colors is wide enough for even the most adventurous gardener. They last for many years in a pot, increasing in beauty every year.

PLANT TYPE Hardy perennial; needs protection below 23°F (−5°C)

HEIGHT 6 in–3 ft 3 in (15 cm–1 m) in a pot

SPREAD 12–24 in (30–60 cm) in a pot

POT SIZE One plant per 12 in- (30 cm-) diameter pot

CALENDAR

	WINTER	SPRING	SUMMER	FALL
IN LEAF				
IN FLOWER				

COLOR

LEAVES Deep green, sometimes variegated

FLOWERS White, yellow, orange, red, pink, purple, bicolored

Buy Peruvian lilies as potted plants as they establish quickly when planted.

CHOOSE

Peruvian lilies vary hugely in height, from the low, spreading Inca Series and Princess Series, less than 12 in (30 cm) high, to the Inticancha Series at 16 in (40 cm) and the Summer Paradise Series that can reach 3 ft 3 in (1 m). The color range includes everything except blue. SUMMER BREEZE has orange flowers above bronze foliage. All these bloom continually through the summer.

INDIAN SUMMER makes mounds of bronze foliage and bright orange flowers.

The shortest kinds of Peruvian lily are perfect for window boxes; taller kinds will supply cut flowers for the house.

PERFECT PARTNERS Plant Peruvian lilies in their own pots, placed beside other bright summer flowers, and among striking foliage plants. **LARGE** *Canna, Lathyrus odorata, Olea europaea* **MEDIUM** *Agapanthus, Nerium oleander, Penstemon* **SMALL** *Dianthus, Heuchera, Lavandula*

PLANT

These plants dislike root disturbance, so they should only be planted as small, growing plants and not as dried roots in packs. Buy growing plants and pot them into enriched potting mix.

To protect the crowns from frost, insulate the pots with bubble wrap (see p.33) and plant the lilies about 2 in (5 cm) deeper than they were in their original pots. To ensure they are established before winter, plant in spring and summer. Young spring shoots are damaged by frost, so protect young plants if they were bought and planted in early spring.

GROW

Young plants will produce upright stems with no flowers. As they establish, each shoot will carry a flower cluster. Keep plants moist and feed once a week. Remove flowered stems by twisting and pulling them from the soil. If left, they will die and spoil the look of the plant.

MAINTAIN After the first hard frost of fall, the foliage will collapse and should be trimmed off. The pots can be left outside but protected from excess wet and cold. A covering of fleece is usually sufficient for this.

When the pot is filled with roots and stems, repot into a larger pot. Plants can be divided by chopping into two or three large clumps in spring but they are best when not disturbed.

BIDENS
BIDENS FERULIFOLIA

Bidens' wiry stems, with their ferny leaves and daisylike flowers, spread among other plants and over the edge of pots. Traditionally yellow, new varieties have more compact habit as well as flowers in orange, white, and pink. All are long-flowering and bring color and wildlife to your patio.

PLANT TYPE Half-hardy perennial, grown as half-hardy annual; needs protection from frost
HEIGHT Up to 8 in (20 cm) in a pot
SPREAD Up to 12 in (30 cm) in a pot
POT SIZE Three plants per 12 in- (30 cm-) diameter pot
☼ ☀

CALENDAR

	WINTER	SPRING	SUMMER	FALL
IN LEAF				
IN FLOWER				

COLOR

LEAVES Deep green, finely divided
FLOWERS Yellow, orange, white, or pink

GROW

Once established, keep the plants moist and feed them every week to maintain growth. Deadheading will ensure they are tidy. Plants will be more compact and flower best in full sun, but they are also useful for part-shaded sites.

MAINTAIN After several months, you may need to cut back the plants to promote new growth if they fail to make new flowers. Bidens are usually discarded at the end of the summer, but cuttings root easily and young plants can be overwintered in a light, frost-free environment.

Bidens' bright yellow blooms are ideal in wall planters. and hanging baskets.

CHOOSE

The original *B. ferulifolia*, with its bright green leaves and rich yellow flowers, is rarely seen today, and has gradually been replaced by more compact cultivars with a wider range of colors. 'Pink Princess' and 'Pretty in Pink' are the most recent, with pink flowers that are a deeper shade in the center, around the yellow "eye." Newer orange kinds include the Bee Series, Bee Happy Series, and Beedance Series. The Sundrop Series has vibrant yellow flowers on compact plants.

PERFECT PARTNERS Bidens combine well with other summer flowers in pots, window boxes, and baskets. The sunny flowers suit fiery color schemes. **LARGE** Canna, Nerium oleander, Olea europaea **MEDIUM** Dahlia, Lilium, Pelargonium **SMALL** Begonia, Calibrachoa, Lysimachia nummularia 'Aurea'

PLANT

Bidens are usually sold as small potted plants or plug plants. They are sensitive to overwatering when young and in cold temperatures; keep them well away from frost. Plant bidens around the edge of pots because of their bushy, trailing habit; they are excellent in window boxes and hanging baskets. Their small leaves and bushy habit also make them suitable for exposed sites.

Keep plants neat and tidy by pinching off flower heads as the petals drop.

DAHLIA *DAHLIA*

Dahlias are loved for their colorful flowers in a variety of shapes and sizes: they can be giants or dwarfs and the most popular have dusky, purple foliage. They flower all summer until the first frost of fall and, if you give them sun and plenty of water, they will delight you for months.

PLANT TYPE Half-hardy, tuberous perennial; needs protection below 41°F (5°C) when growing and 32°F (0°C) when dormant

HEIGHT 8 in–4 ft 9 in (20–150 cm) in a pot

SPREAD 8 in–36 in (20–90 cm) in a pot

POT SIZE One to five plants per 12 in- (30 cm-) diameter pot, depending on cultivar; tall kinds need 16 in- (40 cm-) diameter pots

CALENDAR

	WINTER	SPRING	SUMMER	FALL
IN LEAF				
IN FLOWER				

COLOR

LEAVES Green

FLOWERS White, cream, yellow, gold, orange, red, pink, purple, or lavender; many bicolors

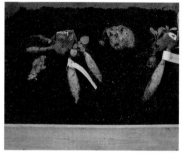

Start dormant tubers in shallow pots or boxes, in warmth, to plant out later.

CHOOSE

Dahlias are available in a wide range of types, sizes, and colors. Among dwarf dahlias, the Dahlietta Series offers dainty, double flowers on compact plants. The Gallery Series has full-size flowers on compact plants about 18 in (45 cm) high in a range of colors. The Happy Single Series has large, single flowers and dark leaves; the

Bishop Series has dark purple leaves and grows about 3 ft 3 in (1 m) high. 'Bishop of Llandaff' is the most popular of these.

PERFECT PARTNERS With such a great variety of plant and flower sizes, dahlias can be dainty window-box plants or vibrant showstoppers in a jungle display. **LARGE** *Canna, Ensete ventricosum, Miscanthus sinensis* **MEDIUM** *Alstroemeria, Lathyrus odoratus, Lilium* **SMALL** *Osteospermum, Pelargonium, Petunia*

PLANT

You can buy dahlias as dried tubers and plant them in potting soil in late spring, about 3 in (8 cm) deep. Or start them into growth in early spring, potted in a warm, bright place away from frost. You can split the tubers, once in growth, into sections, each with a shoot.

Dwarf dahlias can also be grown from seed, sown in warmth in early spring. They will form tubers that you can keep for another year. You can also buy growing plants in summer for immediate results. Dahlias should not be planted out until the danger of frost has passed.

GROW

Dahlias like a sunny spot and lots of water and feeding. Too little water will result in poor growth and lack of flowers. Young dahlia shoots are very prone to attack from slugs and snails. Pinch out the growing tip of tall dahlias once the plants are about 6 in (15 cm) high, to make them bush out and produce more flowers. In windy sites, tall dahlias may need staking. As flowers fade, cut them off, along with their stalks, to prevent seed formation and keep plants looking neat.

MAINTAIN In fall, frost will kill the foliage. Cut back the plants to 3 in (8 cm) and remove them from the pot. Dry the tubers in a cool place and shake off the potting mix. Keep the dry tubers in a cool spot, such as a frost-free shed. Storing in newspaper in a cardboard box is usually effective—do not use plastic, which will cause them to rot.

Larger dahlias make a bold show on their own in pots, and bloom all summer.

TWINFLOWER *DIASCIA*

In recent years, twinflowers have been transformed from an alpine speciality into popular summer flowers everyone can enjoy. These dainty plants with elegant blooms in a range of pastel colors, are perfect for baskets, window boxes, and to cover the edges of pots with flowers all summer.

PLANT TYPE Half-hardy perennial, usually treated as a half-hardy annual
HEIGHT 6–16 in (15–40 cm) in a pot
SPREAD 8–12 in (20–30 cm) in a pot
POT SIZE Three plants per 12 in- (30 cm-) diameter pot
☼ ☼

CALENDAR

COLOR
LEAVES Green
FLOWERS Pink, white, salmon, coral, orange, lilac

	WINTER	SPRING	SUMMER	FALL
IN LEAF				
IN FLOWER				

White twinflowers, Asiatic lilies, and striped grasses combine beautifully.

Their dainty blooms and neat habit make twinflowers ideal for table-top pots.

CHOOSE

Twinflowers are delightful, elegant plants covered in masses of small flowers. Varieties change every year, and groups differ according to habit: some are low and spreading, while others are taller and more upright.

The Diamond Series, which comes in a range of colors, is low and spreading, and the Towers of Flowers Series and Sundiascia Series have tall flower spikes.

LITTLE DANCER is a vigorous grower with pastel pink blooms, while PICCADILLY DENIM BLUE has lavender-colored flowers that fade to a unique smoky blue.

PERFECT PARTNERS Twinflowers associate well with any plants that have colorful foliage and with almost all summer flowers. **LARGE** *Phormium, Salix integra* 'Hakuro-nishiki', *Trachelospermum jasminoides* **MEDIUM** *Alstroemeria, Lavandula, Penstemon* **SMALL** *Carex oshimensis, Dianthus, Heuchera*

PLANT

Young twinflowers are available in the springtime, either as plug plants or as small pots that are ready to put into your patio containers. Their young growth is brittle and easily damaged, so take care when handling the plants.

Pot into commercial potting mix, either with other diascias or mixed with other plants. Twinflowers are suitable for baskets, planters, and window boxes. They are particularly sensitive to overwatering when young and are damaged by frost.

GROW

Keep twinflowers watered and feed every week. Young plants are keen to flower, but pinching out their tips will encourage branching and fuller plants. If allowed to dry out, they can be prone to aphids. Each stem produces a slender stem with dozens of flowers as it extends. When the last flowers have dropped, cut back the stems into the leafy parts to encourage new shoots.

MAINTAIN By late summer, plants can appear to have flowered so much that they make no new growth. At this stage, prune them back hard, removing all flowered shoots and most foliage; feed them and they will produce new growth and blooms. They will continue to bloom after the first frost, but are usually discarded in fall. Plants can be left in pots over winter and may survive mild winters. Trim back in spring and they will burst into new growth.

DAYLILY *HEMEROCALLIS*

The colorful blooms of daylilies last just one day, but stems produce many buds so plants remain colorful for weeks. Their slender, arching leaves are attractive all summer. Yellow is the most common flower color, but there are now countless others to suit every taste and garden style.

PLANT TYPE Hardy, herbaceous perennial
HEIGHT 12–39 in (30–100 cm) in a pot
SPREAD 12–30 in (30–75 cm) in a pot
POT SIZE One plant per 12 in- (30 cm-) diameter pot; needs a larger pot when mature

CALENDAR

	WINTER		SPRING		SUMMER		FALL	
IN LEAF								
IN FLOWER								

COLOR

LEAVES Mid green
FLOWERS Cream, yellow, orange, purple, pink, red many bicolors

GROW

Established plants should produce flower stems from early summer. Keep plants well watered. Flower stems rarely need support. The flowers only last a day and old blooms usually drop off, but may need picking off. When the last bud on the stem has bloomed, cut off the stem as low as possible.

MAINTAIN After the fall frosts, the foliage will yellow and die. Cut down dead foliage to about 3 in (8 cm). Plants can be left outside all winter. If the plant is a few years old and the crown has expanded, with shoots near the edge of the pot, it is time to divide the plant and repot it. Remove it from the pot, chop the clump into three with a spade, and replant one clump per pot.

CHOOSE

There are thousands of varieties of daylily, many of which are available from garden centers; but a few of them remain stubbornly popular. 'Stella de Oro', for example, is compact with yellow flowers, while 'Golden Chimes' has small, yellow flowers flushed with red. The EveryDaylily Series includes many colors on compact plants that are ideal for containers. Several are fragrant, a few have variegated leaves: GOLDEN ZEBRA is the best of these, with deep yellow flowers. Some of the new kinds of double-flowered daylilies need very warm weather to open fully.

PERFECT PARTNERS Daylilies are robust plants with imposing leaves; they combine well with other plants that have large, attractive foliage. **LARGE** *Canna, Melianthus major, Musa basjoo* **MEDIUM** *Alstroemeria, Hosta, Sarcococca* **SMALL** *Agapanthus, Hakonechloa macra, Heuchera*

PLANT

Plants of flowering size are usually sold and can be planted at any time of year. Use an enriched potting mix, which is suitable for long-lasting plants. Large plants in large pots can be surrounded by small bedding plants in the same pot for summer; bulbs can be added for spring interest. Small, bare-root plants bought online can be put in small pots, but should not be crowded by other plants until well established.

'Golden Chimes' is a reliable daylily with bright flowers and arching foliage.

Daylilies bloom in an array of glorious colors and for a month or more.

LANTANA *LANTANA CAMARA*

Lantanas are bright and colorful shrubs that bloom for months in summer. Their crowded heads of small flowers, in numerous pastel shades, are hugely attractive to butterflies. Young plants can be added to baskets and window boxes, while tall specimens make showy focal points in large pots.

PLANT TYPE Tender, evergreen shrub; needs protection below 41°F (5°C)

HEIGHT 12–24 in (30–60 cm) in a pot; can be trained into taller specimens

SPREAD 12–18 in (30–45 cm) in a pot

POT SIZE One plant per 12 in- (30 cm-) diameter pot

 ☼

CALENDAR

	WINTER	SPRING	SUMMER	FALL
IN LEAF				
IN FLOWER				

COLOR

LEAVES Mid-green

FLOWERS White, cream, yellow, orange, pink, red, or mauve

Bright lantanas bring a touch of the Mediterranean to a sunny wall.

CHOOSE

Lantana camara is a vibrant, densely flowered plant, evocative of the Mediterranean region. It thrives in sunny, sheltered spots and is ideal for containers. Most lantanas are bred from *L. camara*, but its hybrids are much bushier, with a wider range of colors. Both the Luscious Series and Lucky Series have compact growth and colors include bright and pastel shades. The most popular are those with two-colored clusters, the flowers changing colors as they age.

PERFECT PARTNERS Bushy lantanas can swamp smaller plants; their appearance suits jungle planting schemes. **LARGE** *Cordyline australis, Olea europaea* **MEDIUM** *Aeonium arboreum, Agapanthus, Melianthus major,* **SMALL** *Calibrachoa, Osteospermum, Pelargonium*

PLANT

Buy young plants in spring after the risk of frost has passed. Small plants dislike waterlogging and cold conditions, so make sure that the plants are well established in their small pots before planting. These plants are ideal for window boxes and hanging baskets. Pinch out the growing tips to encourage branching from low down and more flowers later. Large, specimen plants are often pot-bound, in small pots, and require careful watering to avoid drying out, as well as a stout stake.

GROW

Lantanas thrive in enriched potting mix. Keep them watered and feed with a high-potash fertilizer weekly. Cut off old flower clusters for neatness and to prevent seed formation—they can seed and be invasive in warm climates, but this is not a problem in cooler regions.

Flowers change color as they age, giving a bicolored effect to flower heads.

MAINTAIN Lantanas bloom continuously until their foliage is killed by frosts. If they are in the same pot with other plants that may die off, you can keep them another year by removing them from the pot before they are frosted; pot into enriched potting mix and keep in a cool greenhouse or conservatory in good light. Trim back the stems to remove some foliage and do not let them dry out. As new growth begins in spring, water more frequently and prune off any dead and weak stems.

LILY *LILIUM*

These plants introduce glamour and sophistication to any garden. Each bulb produces a single, upright stem with six-petaled blooms in a variety of shapes and sizes. Lilies flower from early summer to early fall and come in a dazzling array of colors; some flowers are heavily fragrant.

PLANT TYPE Hardy bulb

HEIGHT 18 in–6 ft 6 in (45 cm–2 m) in a pot

SPREAD 6–12 in (15–30 cm) in a pot

POT SIZE Three to five bulbs per 16 in- (40 cm-) diameter pot; tall varieties need larger pots

CALENDAR

	WINTER	SPRING	SUMMER	FALL
IN LEAF				
IN FLOWER				

COLOR

LEAVES Light to dark green

FLOWERS White, pink, red, purple, yellow, orange

GROW

Keep planted bulbs moist. When shoots appear, you can plant the top of the pot with other plants for lower color. Feed weekly with high-potash fertilizer. Lilies rarely need staking, apart from the tallest kinds. If picking stems for the house, leave back at least half the stem to nourish the bulb. When flowers fade, remove the seed pods and let the leaves die down in fall naturally.

MAINTAIN Lilies are hardy, so leave pots outside in winter, as long as they are not waterlogged. After two years, the bulbs may need to be divided—this is best done in early spring or late fall. Lilies are attacked by bright red lily beetles, which must be controlled. Aphids also attack them and spread virus diseases that slowly kill the plants.

CHOOSE

The earliest-flowering lilies are Asiatic types with scentless, upward-facing flowers. Some are dwarfs, ideal for pots. Many are pollen-free (lily pollen is harmful to some cats). The fragrant Oriental types, mostly in white, pink, and red, need lime-free soil and vary in height. Oriental Trumpet Lilies (also known as Orienpet, OT Lilies, Tree Lilies, and Skyscraper Lilies) are tall and need large containers.

PERFECT PARTNERS The huge variety of lilies means they will brighten most plant groupings in summer; they are also great with any evergreens that are dull in summer. **LARGE** *Acer palmatum, Melianthus major, Pseudopanax* **MEDIUM** *Astelia, Euphorbia, Rosa* **SMALL** *Dryopteris erythrosora, Hosta, Pelargonium*

PLANT

Lilies can be bought as dormant bulbs in spring or growing in containers in summer. Plant the bulbs immediately after buying them as they dislike drying out. They produce roots from their stems below soil level, so be sure to plant them 4–6 in (10–15 cm) deep. To prevent the flowers from being crowded in their pots, allow at least 4 in (10 cm) between the bulbs. Lilies are hardy, so if you plant them outside in containers from March onward, they will require no special attention.

Bring pots of lilies in bloom onto the patio for a boost of color and scent.

Bulbs are usually planted in spring and bloom within a few months.

DAFFODIL *NARCISSUS*

Daffodils are readily available, easy to grow, and bring life to gardens after the cold of winter. They are also great value and highly varied. Being subtle or showy, there is a daffodil for every taste: from delicate gems to taller kinds for cutting, and in a multitude of shades and colors.

PLANT TYPE Hardy, spring-flowering bulb
HEIGHT 6–24 in (15–60 cm) in a pot
SPREAD 2–4 in (5–10 cm) in a pot
POT SIZE Six to ten bulbs per 12 in- (30 cm-) diameter pot
☼ ◑

CALENDAR

	WINTER	SPRING	SUMMER	FALL
IN LEAF		▓▓	▒	
IN FLOWER		▓		

COLOR

LEAVES Blue-green or green

FLOWERS White, cream, yellow, orange, pink (salmon-pink); often bicolored

Miniature daffodils should be planted in early fall to bloom in spring.

'Elka', a miniature daffodil, flowers early and can be left in pots for years.

CHOOSE

The best daffodil for pots is 'Tête-à-tête', a reliable, early-flowering dwarf. Its counterpart is the double daffodil 'Tête Bouclé'. Other good, short daffodils are 'February Gold', yellow and orange 'Jetfire', creamy white 'Elka', and the primrose-yellow 'Hawera'. White and cream 'Ice Follies' is taller and more vigorous.

PERFECT PARTNERS Daffodils can be planted in permanent pots with shrubs, combined with spring flowers in pots, or used to fill window boxes and upscaled containers **LARGE** *Acer palmatum, Hedera, Laurus nobilis* **MEDIUM** *Buxus sempervirens, Carex, Erysimum* **SMALL** *Helleborus, Heuchera, Hosta*

PLANT

Plant daffodil bulbs in late September or October. Planting depth is 2½ times the height of the bulb, so a 2 in- (5 cm-) tall bulb would need planting with its top 5 in (12 cm) below the surface. This is only critical if the bulbs are to stay in the pots for longer than one winter. It means that they will be deep enough in the pot to allow overplanting without being damaged. Using enriched potting mix, plant the daffodils close together for a really dramatic display, but space them out as much as 3 in (8 cm) apart for long-term containers.

GROW

Keep your pots moist after planting the bulbs—this is especially important for double daffodils, which can have dead buds if they are left to dry out. They do not need protection from frost.

Use liquid fertilizer during spring to feed the daffodils and any other spring plants in the pot. Remove any dead flowers and the seed pods, to prevent seed formation, and allow the foliage to die down naturally.

MAINTAIN If you want to change your containers during summer, allow the foliage to turn yellow before removing the bulbs from the pots. Dry off the bulbs and then replant them in fall. Alternatively, they can be left in the same pots to bloom for the next year.

NEMESIA *NEMESIA*

Shrubby nemesias are compact plants that flower all summer in a wide range of glorious colors. Their dainty flowers are sweetly scented and produced so freely that they cover the plants. They are quick into bloom and are also among the hardiest summer bedding plants.

PLANT TYPE Half-hardy, shrubby perennial, usually grown as half-hardy annual
HEIGHT Up to 8 in (20 cm) in a pot
SPREAD Up to 8 in (20 cm) in a pot
POT SIZE Three plants per 12 in- (30 cm-) diameter pot
☀ ☀

CALENDAR

	WINTER	SPRING	SUMMER	FALL
IN LEAF				
IN FLOWER				

COLOR

LEAVES Green
FLOWERS Lilac, purple, white, wine red, yellow, or blue; many bicolors

Young plug plants need growing on in small pots before planting in patio pots.

Bushy and compact, nemesia flowers so freely that its leaves are barely visible.

CHOOSE

New cultivars and colors of nemesia are introduced every year, often with two-colored blooms. Even so, 'Wisley Vanilla', a traditional favorite, remains staunchly popular because its cream flowers are so intensely fragrant.

Other good options include the Sundae Series, with bicolored blooms; in the Aroma Series, with blooms in vibrant colors combined with yellow, AROMA RHUBARB AND CUSTARD and AROMA PLUMS and CUSTARD are popular. The lavender-colored 'Mirabelle' and dark blue MYRTILLE have masses of smaller flowers.

PERFECT PARTNERS Being compact and rather dumpy, nemesias contrast well with plants that have flowing forms. **LARGE** *Clematis, Miscanthus sinensis, Salix integra* 'Hakuro-nishiki' **MEDIUM** *Begonia, Fuchsia, Hakonechloa macra, Lantana* **SMALL** *Festuca glauca, Verbena*

PLANT

Nemesias are most often sold as small plants in 3 in (8 cm) pots, ready to plant out in late spring. Plug plants are also available and need to be potted into small pots and grown on before planting out. Young, tender plants are prone to frost damage and must be protected. They can be planted in commercial potting mix.

GROW

Keep plants watered, and feed once a week. Bushy plants produce dozens of stems with clusters of flowers, which remain in bloom for many weeks. When the last flowers drop on each stem, trim them off, cutting back to a pair of healthy leaves. This will encourage new growth and more flowers in two or three weeks' time. Well-fed plants will flower more profusely with each flush of growth

MAINTAIN Plants are often discarded at the end of fall, but mature plants will survive light frosts and live into the next year. Younger nemesias can be left in pots if they are planted with shrubs and perennials—in this case, they may be able to survive mild winters. If they do survive, you can prune the plants back hard in spring to tidy any damaged stems and promote new growth.

CAPE DAISY *OSTEOSPERMUM*

These daisylike summer flowers, traditionally white or purple, are available in a host of different colors, including pastel shades that lend themselves to adventurous planting plans. The flowers open most reliably in a sunny spot and the bushy, compact plants withstand a little drought.

PLANT TYPE Half-hardy perennial; may survive mild winters outside, but needs protection below 41°F (5°C)

HEIGHT 8–16 in (20–40 cm) in a pot, depending on type

SPREAD 12–16 in (30–40 cm) in a pot

POT SIZE One plant per 12 in- (30 cm-) diameter pot

CALENDAR

	WINTER	SPRING	SUMMER	FALL
IN LEAF				
IN FLOWER				

COLOR

LEAVES Deep green

FLOWERS White, pink, purple, yellow, peach, or orange

Cape daisies will be in full bloom when planted and will continue all summer.

CHOOSE

The range of Cape daisies changes yearly, but older kinds such as 'Pink Whirls' remain popular, while new doubles, including the 3D Series, stay open even in cloudy weather, unlike older kinds that only opened in full sun.

The Serenity Series includes bright and pastel colors; the plants are compact and bloom well into the fall.

PERFECT PARTNERS Cape daisies make a magnificent display on their own but can be planted with other sun lovers in the same pot; they are reliable and flower for many months. **LARGE** *Laurus nobilis*, *Salix integra* 'Hakuro-nishiki', *Trachelospermum jasminoides* **MEDIUM** *Euphorbia*, *Phormium* **SMALL** *Heliotropium arborescens*, *Pelargonium*, *Verbena*

PLANT

Young plants can be bought in late spring and added to pots. Mature plants withstand light frost but the young plants are frost-sensitive. They are also intolerant of wet potting soil when small, so plant and water sparingly at first, especially in cool, wet weather. Cape daisies are useful mixed with short-lived plants such as lobelia because they will continue to grow and bloom and cover any gaps later in the season.

GROW

Make sure plants are moist and feed them once a week to promote growth. Keep them neat by cutting off faded flowers at the base of the stalk. They can be prone to aphid attack, so check them regularly and rub off the pests. Pinching out is not necessary with modern varieties that are naturally bushy. Keep the pots in full sun to maintain bushy growth and lots of blooms—shade can cause straggly growth and lack of flowers.

MAINTAIN Prune Cape daisies in late summer if they are getting too large and they will bloom again. To keep plants for next year, take cuttings in late summer and store them free from frost over winter. Old plants can sometimes survive winter outside in urban and coastal areas.

The daisylike flowers are produced all summer in a range of pastel colors.

PENSTEMON *PENSTEMON*

These neat, upright plants can be relied on to produce masses of tubular blooms in a wide range of colors throughout summer. Easy to grow and maintain, penstemons are usually at their best in late summer and will keep your containers packed with bloom right into fall.

PLANT TYPE Hardy, shrubby perennial; needs protection below 32°F (0°C) in exposed gardens
HEIGHT 16 in–30 in (40–75 cm) in a pot
SPREAD 12–18 in (30–45 cm) in a pot
POT SIZE One to three plants per 12 in- (30 cm-) diameter pot
☼ ☼

CALENDAR

	WINTER	SPRING	SUMMER	FALL
IN LEAF		▓▓	▓▓	▓▓
IN FLOWER			▓▓	▓▓

COLOR

LEAVES Green
FLOWERS White, pink, red, purple, mauve, or lilac; many bicolors with white

CHOOSE

Most penstemons are bought as plants, but they can also be grown from seed. Traditional favorites include 'White Bedder', red 'Andenken an Friedrich Hahn' and 'Schoenholzeri', rose-pink 'Hidcote Pink', and the purple 'Raven'.

The wonderfully vibrant Pensham Series also offers great options, with white-throated blooms that come in a multitude of colors, including the pink 'Pensham Laura', purple 'Pensham Czar', and the cherry-red 'Pensham Amelia Jane'.

PERFECT PARTNERS With such a wide range of appealing colors available, penstemons are ideal for mixed plantings in large containers, where they provide height and contrast to bushy and trailing summer plants. **LARGE** *Clematis, Olea europaea, Rosa* **MEDIUM** *Euphorbia, Fuchsia, Melianthus major* **SMALL** *Heliotropium arborescens, Nemesia, Petunia*

PLANT

Penstemons are usually bought as small plants in spring or mature plants in bloom in summer. Small plants need protection from frost in spring.

These plants should last you for several years before they need replacing, so plant them in organically enriched potting mix to help ensure a longer plant life. Pinch out the tips of young plants so that they bush out first before starting to bloom.

'Andenken an Friedrich Hahn' is a hardy, smaller-flowered penstemon.

GROW

Penstemons grow quickly and need plenty of water and feeding. When growing well, new, upright stems are produced that end in spires of blooms. These open over many weeks; when they have all faded, cut off the stem back to a pair of leaves so that new shoots replace these. Toward fall, some lower leaves will turn brown and may need to be removed.

MAINTAIN Although generally hardy, extreme cold may kill penstemons. Cover plants in exposed gardens with fleece in the dead of winter. You can take cuttings of nonflowering shoots in late summer—they root easily. In spring, cut back mature plants to keep them neat and promote new growth.

Penstemons are readily propagated by tip cuttings taken in late summer.

FRENCH MARIGOLD

TAGETES PATULA

The common French marigold is easy, bright, and reliable, and if you grow it from seed, you can enjoy unusual kinds not seen in garden centers. The plant's pungent leaves repulse some and delight others—but whatever the verdict, these neat, colorful plants are sure to enliven your garden.

PLANT TYPE Half-hardy annual; needs protection below 41°F (5°C)

HEIGHT 6–8 in (15–20 cm), taller in some varieties

SPREAD 6–8 in (15–20 cm), taller in some varieties

POT SIZE Six plants per 12 in- (30 cm-) diameter pot

☼

CALENDAR

	WINTER	SPRING	SUMMER	FALL
IN LEAF				
IN FLOWER				

COLOR

LEAVES Dark green, with red stems

FLOWERS Cream, mahogany red, orange, tangerine, yellow, gold

French marigolds thrive in a sunny spot but bloom even in a wet summer.

CHOOSE

If buying from a garden center, French marigolds will probably not be named and will be in traditional orange shades.

These are easy plants to grow from seed and they flower quickly, so they are worth trying, even on a windowsill indoors. Growing from seed opens up a wider range of color options: an old favorite, 'Naughty Marietta', has single yellow flowers with maroon blotches; 'Striped Marvel' is tall and bushy with striped petals; 'Strawberry Blonde' has red, yellow, and blush-pink flowers.

PERFECT PARTNERS French marigolds are cheerful and unpretentious—ideal for children, cottage gardens, and fiery color schemes. **LARGE** *Canna, Cordyline australis, Ipomoea tricolor* **MEDIUM** *Erysimum, Lilium, Penstemon* **SMALL** *Bidens, Lobelia erinus, Lysimachia nummularia* 'Aurea'

PLANT

French marigolds must be protected from frost in spring. Buy packs of plants and plant into pots, with commercial potting mix, about 4–6 in (10–15 cm) apart, depending on how long you are prepared to wait for them to "fill in." Make sure they are well watered before and after planting. Pinching out the first flower, which is often present when buying, will help the plants become better established.

Single types, like 'Naughty Marietta', are showy, easy to grow, and inexpensive.

GROW

Protect your French marigolds from slugs and snails, which will eat whole plants overnight. Keep the plants well watered, and feed them weekly to promote growth and flowers. Plants in part shade will grow, but they will flower less freely. The spicy-tasting flower petals are edible.

MAINTAIN As the flowers fade, snap off the blooms in order to prevent seed formation and keep the plants looking neat. In extremely wet spells, the flowers may rot, so these should be removed. French marigolds are annuals and should be pulled up and composted at the end of the fall.

A plant grouping in a shaded area needs care to arrange, but there are many shade-loving plants with gorgeous flowers and foliage, such as these stunning hellebores, which bloom in early spring.

FOR SHADE

Having a shady patio may limit the range of plants you can grow, but it will not stop you creating vibrant, eye-catching displays—many shade lovers are beautiful plants that will brighten even the most gloomy corner.

COPING WITH SHADE

Most plants that grow in shade have dark green leaves and many are evergreen. This means that they have evolved to survive in dimly lit woodland, retaining their foliage in winter so that they can make the most of the light after the trees above lose their leaves. In the garden border, shade under trees is a problem because the soil is often full of roots, impoverished, and dry. But if shade-loving plants are grown in pots, they get all the water and nutrients they need to grow to perfection.

WINTER DISPLAYS

Many shade-loving plants not only have leaves in winter but flowers, too. You can enjoy these blooms—in their pots in the garden or patio—from the house, when it is too cold to venture out. Lenten roses are the stars of winter displays, with enormous variation in flower color. Bring them to the fore in winter, when in bloom, and tuck them among other plants in summer, where they will cope with the shade.

Camellias are among the most popular of all patio plants, loved for their glossy leaves and sumptuous blooms in late winter and spring. The shelter of a shaded patio suits them well and helps protect their delicate blooms from late-spring frosts.

SLOW-GROWING, LONG-LIVED

Shade lovers tend to grow slowly, which is a major advantage on the patio as it reduces the need to repot and prune (though they will need to be fed and watered, of course). Japanese maples, one of the most popular shrubs for patio pots, can live for decades, increasing in beauty every year. Boxwood, whether clipped into cones or balls, can be kept healthy in pots for many years, giving much-needed structure to your planting. The lily turf (*Liriope muscari*) is a useful feature plant or ground cover in pots with deciduous shrubs, such as maples; it slowly increases in size every year and needs little attention, and has the added bonus of colorful flowers in fall. For impatient gardeners, there is variegated greater periwinkle, a colorful plant that brightens the dullest corner with its enthusiastic growth.

JAPANESE MAPLE *ACER PALMATUM*

These elegant, small trees are ideal for part-shaded patios. They combine longevity, hardiness, and slow growth with an array of spectacular leaf colors. Japanese maples become more attractive as they mature and, at their best, will become the pride of your patio display.

PLANT TYPE Hardy, deciduous tree
HEIGHT Up to 6 ft 6 in (2 m) in a pot
SPREAD Up to 4 ft 9 in (1.5 m) in a pot
POT SIZE One plant per 12 in- (30 cm-) diameter pot
☼ ☼

CALENDAR

	WINTER	SPRING	SUMMER	FALL
IN LEAF				
IN FLOWER				

COLOR

LEAVES Lime green, green, wine-red, variegated, or orange-flushed

FLOWERS Tiny, red-green

CHOOSE

Japanese maples have been loved for centuries, which means there are plenty of cultivars to choose from. The most basic have leaves divided into five or seven narrow lobes and, among these, are many variations in leaf color. These Japanese maples are the easiest to grow and most resistant to conditions such as strong sunlight and wind. In this group you will find the red-leaved "Trompenburg" and 'Garnet', and the apricot-colored 'Orange Dream'. 'Sango-kaku' is popular for its bright spring foliage and yellow fall color, the leaves dropping to reveal coral-red stems that are bright all winter.

Other maples have intricately divided leaves, typified by 'Dissectum', which has green or purple leaves. These are slower growing; have a lower, spreading habit; and are more sensitive to poor growing conditions, the threadlike leaves "crisping" in dry weather. Between these types are several other forms, many with variegated leaves edged with white and pink. All have stunning fall hues, the leaves turning rich colors before they drop.

PERFECT PARTNERS Much of the charm of Japanese maples is their elegant habit, so they look especially good with subtle flowers and attractive foliage that do not detract from their leaves. Because they prefer a part-shaded spot, they can provide the perfect conditions for shade-loving plants. **LARGE** Camellia, Phyllostachys nigra, Viburnum tinus **MEDIUM** Dryopteris erythrosora, Hosta, Pseudopanax lessonii **SMALL** Carex, Hakonechloa macra, Liriope spicata

'Orange Dream' is a popular choice because of its rich, golden and red foliage throughout summer and its vibrant fall color.

The bright red spring foliage of 'Trompenburg' becomes greener in summer but transforms into flaming orange in fall.

PLANT

Japanese maples can be planted at any time if bought growing in pots. Planting in summer, when the plants are in full leaf, will require vigilance to prevent drying out and subsequent leaf scorch.

Plants are available in a range of sizes. If buying small, inexpensive plants in 3½ in (9 cm) pots, these should be planted into 8 in- (20 cm-) intermediate pots for two years before being moved into their permanent, ornamental pots. This will prevent the small plant being surrounded by wet potting mix, causing root damage. They prefer an acid soil but are not as sensitive to lime as camellias (see p.109). Use lime-free potting mix with added organic matter. Make sure that your chosen pot has straight sides and a wide top to allow for repotting.

Ground-cover plants and spring-flowering bulbs can be planted in the pot for extra color and interest.

A mature Japanese maple will become the highlight of your shady patio.

GROW

Keep these trees moist at all times. Place them in a spot that is protected from strong sun and winds, both of which will damage the foliage, causing the leaf tips to wither. New, spring growth is prone to damage from late spring frosts. This is more likely on plants on patios, where the plants come into growth early because of their shelter and then get damaged by late frosts. If frost does damage new growth, prune this off and new shoots will soon grow. In spring, put a time-release fertilizer around the plants or feed every week with a general liquid fertilizer from late spring to late summer. Japanese maples are rarely affected by pests but aphids may feed on young shoots (see p.36).

The elegant habit of Japanese maples suits minimalist design styles.

MAINTAIN Plants rarely need pruning but branches can be shortened or removed to maintain the desired shape. This is best done in summer, when plants are in full leaf so you can see the results. Pruning can also be carried out in winter, but avoid this task in spring, when the cuts can "bleed" sap.

Japanese maples will require repotting after two or more years in the same containers. When it is not practical to repot, top-dress the pot with fresh potting mix (see p.31) or remove from the pot and cut away the lower portion of the roots and replace with fresh potting mix in the same pot.

Japanese maples drop their leaves in fall and these should be swept up. The plants are hardy and do not need winter protection, but must be kept moist throughout the entire year.

BOXWOOD *BUXUS SEMPERVIRENS*

Tough and tolerant of shade and sun, boxwood is a popular choice for garden topiary and adapts well to life in a container. Its small leaves make it easy to clip into intricate shapes, but it is most often trimmed into cones and balls. The shrub's crisp outline contrasts with lush foliage.

PLANT TYPE Hardy, evergreen shrub
HEIGHT Up to 3 ft 3 in (1 m) in a pot
SPREAD Up to 24 in (60 cm) in a pot
POT SIZE One plant per 12 in- (30 cm-) diameter pot

CALENDAR

	WINTER	SPRING	SUMMER	FALL
IN LEAF				
IN FLOWER				

COLOR

LEAVES Green
FLOWERS Tiny, yellow, insignificant

CHOOSE

The common boxwood, *Buxus sempervirens*, is a large shrub that will introduce formality to any garden or patio. In time, it will grow into a distinctive small tree. It is usually represented by the smaller and bushier cultivar 'Suffruticosa', which is often planted as a low hedge and clipped into small topiary shapes. Both these types of boxwood have the same requirements. Variegated boxwood is always a popular choice, including the white-edged 'Elegantissima' and the striking, yellow-edged 'Gold Tip'.

PERFECT PARTNERS Use this shrub to frame other plants and flowers. **LARGE** *Cordyline australis, Laurus nobilis, Olea europaea* **MEDIUM** *Hemerocallis, Melianthus major, Pelargonium* **SMALL** *Dryopteris erythrosora, Festuca glauca, Hakonechloa macra*

PLANT

Boxwood is usually sold as pre-clipped specimens or in packs of small plants for low hedges. Small plants can be trained, but buying already shaped specimens will save you several years of growing. Plant in enriched potting mix. If planting flowers around it in the same pot, avoid crowding the base of the boxwood plant or its foliage will be shaded and the plant may turn brown and die.

A clipped, standard boxwood is easy to maintain and looks good all year.

GROW

Keep potting mix moist at all times and feed regularly in spring and summer to promote growth. Part shade is best; protect from intense sun. In extreme conditions and if plants are starved, the foliage will turn bronze, but will recover if plants are shaded and fed. Drought causes yellowing and leaf drop—boxwood plants will rarely recover.

MAINTAIN Overgrown plants sprout from the base when hard pruned. Boxwood is susceptible to blight (a fungal disease caused by damp and overcrowding)—remedy by spraying with fungicide or hard pruning. Boxwood caterpillars are also a problem; pick off or spray as soon as they appear.

Keep plants neat by trimming in late spring and then again in late summer.

CAMELLIA *CAMELLIA × WILLIAMSII*

Camellias are popular for their showy flowers in spring. The glossy foliage is attractive all year and can be pruned to stay neat. Growing these plants in a pot means you can move them to a sheltered spot, out of the cold, to protect their blooms, which can be ruined by late spring frosts.

PLANT TYPE Hardy, evergreen shrub

HEIGHT Up to 6 ft 6 in (2 m) in a pot, depending on cultivars

SPREAD Up to 3 ft 3 in (1 m) in a pot, depending on cultivars

POT SIZE One plant per 12 in- (30 cm-) diameter pot

CALENDAR

	WINTER	SPRING	SUMMER	FALL
IN LEAF				
IN FLOWER				

COLOR

LEAVES Dark green

FLOWERS White, cream, pink, red, or dark red

GROW

Keep camellia plants moist at all times and feed in spring and summer. Flower buds appear in late summer, but stop growing completely if plants dry out. Camellias have leathery leaves that do not wilt when soil is dry, so take care that the potting mix is moist all year.

'Donation' is a popular camellia but needs pinching out to stay compact.

CHOOSE

There are hundreds of camellias on the market. The most popular kinds are cultivars of *Camellia japonica* and the hybrid *C. × williamsii*.

The *C. × williamsii* hybrids have the advantage of dropping their old blooms, which keeps them always looking fresh. When in flower, they are likely to outclass almost every other plant on your patio.

The silvery pink 'Donation' and the rich pink 'Debbie' are particularly sought-after. Of the *C. japonica* cultivars, 'Jury's Yellow' is unusual for its yellow blooms.

PERFECT PARTNERS During summer, camellia's glossy foliage provides a terrific background to bright flowers. **LARGE** *Acer palmatum, Hedera colchica, Skimmia japonica* **MEDIUM** *Buxus sempervirens, Hemerocallis, Pseudopanax* **SMALL** *Begonia, Dryopteris erythrosora, Hakonechloa macra*

PLANT

Camellias need lime-free potting mix, so plant them in a mix intended for acid lovers. They can be planted at any time of year but plants are usually available in spring, when they are in bud. Only buy the named varieties because unnamed plants can be inferior and may not bloom freely.

These plants are highly sensitive to drought, so make sure they are well watered, both before taking them out of the containers you originally bought them in and also after planting.

Watch out for sooty mold—a sure sign your plant is infected by scale insect.

MAINTAIN Camellias do not need pruning but you can pinch out the topmost shoot when it starts to grow in spring to encourage bushy growth. The plants are often infested with scale insect if stressed: the insects drip sticky "honeydew" onto lower leaves, which become colonized by "sooty mold" (see p.37). Use insecticide (organic, if preferred) on these pests. Vine weevils can also attack the roots of camellias and eat their foliage (see p.36).

SEDGE *CAREX*

Sedges look similar to ornamental grasses, and are frequently grouped with them, but they are a diverse range of plants, grown for their attractive foliage. Those with variegated, evergreen leaves are most common and valued, especially for introducing fall and winter color.

PLANT TYPE Hardy, evergreen, grasslike plant

HEIGHT Up to 8–16 in (20–40 cm) in a pot, depending on species

SPREAD Up to 8–16 in (20–40 cm) in a pot, depending on species

POT SIZE One plant per 8 in- (20 cm-) diameter pot, three to five plants per 16 in- (40 cm-) diameter pot

CALENDAR

	WINTER	SPRING	SUMMER	FALL
IN LEAF				
IN FLOWER				

COLOR

LEAVES Yellow, green, or brown

FLOWERS Small, brown, insignificant

'Evergold' has elegant, arching, golden leaves with dark green margins.

CHOOSE

The most popular *Carex* have golden variegated leaves that form gorgeous, arching mounds of narrow leaves. *C. oshimensis* 'Evergold' is easy to grow in shade. Two bronze-leaved sedges, *C. comans* and the more upright *C. buchananii*, are useful as a contrast to other plants and flowers but need full sun to thrive. *C. elata* 'Aurea' has bright yellow leaves and prefers part shade and moisture.

PERFECT PARTNERS Variable in form and color, their leaves contrast well with bold foliage; being shade-tolerant, they are also useful for planting under shrubs in pots. **LARGE** *Acer palmatum, Hedera, Laurus nobilis* **MEDIUM** *Buxus sempervirens, Phormium, Sarcococca* **SMALL** *Calluna vulgaris, Hosta, Narcissus*

PLANT

Plant sedges in spring or fall. They are especially useful for winter and spring pots and window boxes. Allow them room to arch and display their foliage elegantly. *C. oshimensis* is very effective in disguising the edges of pots. Always use a good-quality potting mix.

GROW

All types grow best if the potting mix is kept moist—they do not respond well to drought. Feed weekly through spring and summer. Small, often brown flowers are produced on stems above the foliage but are not showy and are usually cut off as soon as they develop.

MAINTAIN If they look shabby, cut off old leaves in spring, before the new flush of foliage. It is often easiest to cut off all the old leaves 2 in (5 cm) above soil level. After several years, clumps can become bare in the center. If this happens, dig up the plants in spring, pull them apart into three or more clumps, and replant them immediately.

Pull apart clumps of sedge in spring; replant them immediately and water well.

EUONYMUS *EUONYMUS FORTUNEI*

Evergreen euonymus are easygoing and tolerant of shade and regular pruning. They also bring bright color to the garden or patio in their variegated forms. These hardy plants are useful to place under large shrubs and between more spectacular plants at any time of year.

PLANT TYPE Hardy, evergreen shrub
HEIGHT Up to 24 in (60 cm) in a pot
SPREAD Up to 24 in (60 cm) in a pot
POT SIZE One plant per 12 in- (30 cm-) diameter pot
☀ ☼

CALENDAR

	WINTER	SPRING	SUMMER	FALL
IN LEAF	▓	▓	▓	▓
IN FLOWER		▓		

COLOR

LEAVES Green, variegated with white or yellow
FLOWERS Cream, insignificant

CHOOSE

Most evergreen euonymus are cultivars of the striking, easy-care *Euonymus fortunei*. White-variegated 'Emerald Gaiety' and yellow 'Emerald 'n' Gold' are bushy and vigorous. 'Harlequin' has leaves that are white when young and speckled with green when mature.

With regular pruning, euonymus will remain neat and colorful all year.

If you are in search of a similar but more upright plant with larger leaves, try *E. japonicus*, which is often variegated with yellow. Both this and *E. fortunei* are suitable for windy, exposed sites.

PERFECT PARTNERS The dense, small foliage of evergreen euonymus is a foil for more dramatic leaves with rounded and spiky shapes; the bright colors of variegated kinds contrast with colorful summer flowers. **LARGE** *Fatsia japonica, Musa basjoo, Trachycarpus fortunei* **MEDIUM** *Dryopteris erythrosora, Phormium* **SMALL** *Begonia, Fuchsia, Heuchera*

PLANT

Euonymus are especially useful for part shady conditions. If clipped, they can be grown as specimens in their own pots but small plants are useful in combination with other plants, especially for winter window boxes and baskets. Use enriched potting mix for large, permanent specimens. *E. japonicus* is often sold as a small standard plant, 24 in (60 cm) high. This needs permanent staking or its rather brittle main stems may snap.

GROW

Variegated euonymus are at their brightest in spring, when their flush of new growth is still young. Keep the plants moist, even in winter, and feed once a week in spring and summer. Established plants produce tiny flowers but these are not showy. Euonymus will thrive in sun or part shade.

MAINTAIN Light pruning in spring and summer will encourage a dense habit. The plants form loose mounds of foliage and, if not trimmed, long stems attach themselves to walls and fences by aerial roots. Euonymus frequently produce all-green or all-yellow shoots, which also need cutting off.

Cut out all-yellow and all-green shoots to maintain a perfect variegated specimen.

LENTEN ROSE *HELLEBORUS × HYBRIDUS*

These plants are valued for their bold foliage in summer and delicate flowers, produced in late winter and spring. They have subtle variations in flower color, which make them particularly collectible and, for some, addictive. If content, Lenten roses will live for many years.

PLANT TYPE Hardy, evergreen perennial
HEIGHT Up to 16 in (40 cm) in a pot
SPREAD Up to 18 in (45 cm) in a pot
POT SIZE One plant per 12 in- (30 cm-) diameter pot

CALENDAR

	WINTER	SPRING	SUMMER	FALL
IN LEAF				
IN FLOWER				

COLOR

LEAVES Dark green
FLOWERS White, pink, red, purple, green, or pale yellow

GROW

Keep Lenten roses moist at all times and feed weekly through spring and summer. As the flowers fade, remove the flower stems, cutting them off at the base. This keeps plants tidy and also prevents seed formation and colonization by aphids (see p.36).

Remove old Lenten rose blooms to prevent seed formation.

CHOOSE

The most popular of all the hellebores are Lenten roses, which have attractive, bold foliage and single and double flowers in a wide range of colors. They are usually grown from seed and are inexpensive and tolerant of part shade.

Other options for similar hellebores include the Christmas rose, *Helleborus niger*, which flowers earlier in spring than the Lenten rose and has white

Buy Lenten roses in bloom to add instant color in the depths of winter.

blooms. Some of the more modern hybrids, such as *H. × glandorfensis*, do not set seed, are especially free-flowering, and have attractive leaves, often marbled with pink or silver.

PERFECT PARTNERS Plant Lenten roses in large pots under deciduous shrubs for winter interest. They mix well with spring bulbs and flowers—the hellebore leaves will cover the dying leaves of spring bulbs. **LARGE** *Acer palmatum*, *Hydrangea anomala* subsp. *petiolaris*, *Salix integra* 'Hakuro-nishiki' **MEDIUM** *Daphne*, *Hemerocallis*, *Melianthus major* **SMALL** *Carex*, *Hakonechloa macra*, *Heuchera*

PLANT

Buy plants in early spring, when in bud or bloom, as this will allow you to choose the color you want. Soak plants well before planting to ensure water will be properly absorbed later by the root ball. Plant in enriched potting mix mixed with time-release fertilizer to sustain growth. They can be combined in large pots with herbaceous plants and grasses for winter interest.

MAINTAIN In winter, the old, unsightly leaves should be cut off at the base, which will prevent any diseases from infecting the new spring foliage and, in addition, will show off the flowers, produced in spring. These plants are long-lived and do not usually need regular division—but, if it is necessary, it should be done in winter, at the same time as cutting off the old leaves.

LILY TURF *LIRIOPE MUSCARI*

The grassy leaves of lily turf form dense clumps of foliage that change little through the year. Spikes of flowers appear in fall—these are usually purple, although white-flowered kinds are also available. Slow-growing and long-lived, lily turf is easy to care for and withstands shade.

PLANT TYPE Hardy, evergreen, herbaceous perennial
HEIGHT Up to 12 in (30 cm) in a pot
SPREAD Up to 12 in (30 cm) in a pot
POT SIZE One plant per 8 in- (20 cm-) diameter pot; three plants per 16 in- (40 cm-) diameter pot
☀ ☼

CALENDAR

	WINTER	SPRING	SUMMER	FALL
IN LEAF				
IN FLOWER				▓ ▓

COLOR

LEAVES Dark green, often variegated
FLOWERS Purple or white

GROW

Keep plants moist at all times and feed throughout spring and summer. They are resistant to drought and some neglect but will look better and grow more rapidly if well looked after. Plants flower best in part shade but they will withstand very shaded conditions. In deep shade, the foliage will be longer and more arching.

MAINTAIN Plants look healthier and neater if groomed in spring by pulling out or cutting off old, dead leaves. The old flower stems should be cut off at the base in winter. Plants become dense after three or four years and can be divided and replanted in spring, but otherwise, little maintenance is needed.

The **stiff spires** of lily turf flowers have a welcome freshness in fall.

CHOOSE

Liriope muscari is mainly grown for its attractive, thick, arching leaves. The most popular kinds include the free-flowering 'Moneymaker' and 'Big Blue'. Variegated lily turfs are more showy and are useful to brighten up shady areas in the garden or patio—they include yellow 'Variegata' and 'Gold-banded' and the cream-edged 'John Burch'. 'Monroe White' has dark green leaves and white flowers.

PERFECT PARTNERS Lily turf flowers in fall but the dark green, strappy leaves are attractive among brighter, small plants in spring and summer. **LARGE** *Fatsia japonica, Ilex aquifolium, Laurus nobilis* **MEDIUM** *Buxus sempervirens, Pseudopanax lessonii, Viburnum davidii* **SMALL** *Helleborus, Heuchera, Vinca major*

PLANT

The plants are usually sold in the fall, when in bloom, but they can be planted at any time of year. They are long-lived and therefore best planted in enriched potting mix.

Lily turfs are perfect for window boxes because as they grow they increase in width but not height. Because they withstand shade and are always neat, they are also ideal for underplanting taller plants in large pots. They can be underplanted with spring bulbs, but as they mature their dense roots will smother the bulbs.

As plants mature, cut out old foliage to leave the clumps clean and tidy.

VIBURNUM *VIBURNUM DAVIDII*

This handsome, low-growing shrub has lustrous, oval leaves with three veins and red leaf stalks. It is low and spreading in habit and has clusters of small, white flowers in summer. If both male and female plants are grown, females produce metallic-blue berries. Viburnum grows well in shade.

PLANT TYPE Hardy, evergreen shrub
HEIGHT Up to 24 in (60 cm) in a pot
SPREAD Up to 30 in (75 cm) in a pot
POT SIZE One plant per 12 in- (30 cm-) diameter pot

CALENDAR

COLOR

LEAVES Dark green
FLOWERS Dull white

	WINTER	SPRING	SUMMER	FALL
IN LEAF				
IN FLOWER				

CHOOSE

This plant is distinctive for its bold foliage and low, spreading habit. Solitary plants will not produce the showy, blue berries, but plants are rarely sold with the sexes labeled; both the male and female are needed for the female to produce berries. If berries are a key feature for you, buy two plants in fall, one with the berries present.

If you are looking for a plant that is similar but taller and looser in habit, try *V. cinnamomifolium*—although this species is not as widely available as *V. davidii* in garden centers.

PERFECT PARTNERS The boldly textured foliage on viburnum's low, spreading growth is useful in shade under large foliage plants, especially those with tall or arching growth. **LARGE** *Acer palmatum*, *Fatsia japonica*, *Trachycarpus fortunei* **MEDIUM** *Buxus sempervirens*, *Phormium*, *Sarcococca*, **SMALL** *Hakonechloa macra*, *Heuchera*, *Liriope muscari*

PLANT

This striking evergreen thrives in part shade, although it will have a looser habit in dense shade. It is better grown in its own pot than in association with other plants because of its spreading habit. Plant in enriched potting mix and keep moist at all times.

In summer, even small plants produce neat clusters of white flowers.

Expect berries in fall and winter if you have both male and female plants.

GROW

Feed your viburnum throughout the spring and summer, as new growth is being produced, and when it is in bloom. Unless you have a female plant capable of producing berries, the old bloom clusters should be cut off for neatness as soon as they fade.

MAINTAIN Prune plants lightly in spring to keep them neat. Make sure they are watered throughout the year, even in winter, when they still need moisture. Leaves may "hang" alarmingly in frosty weather but will recover when they thaw. The foliage is often eaten by vine weevils (see p.36), which make notches around the edge of the leaves. This will not harm the viburnum but is a sign that these pests are in the garden and may attack other, more vulnerable plants.

GREATER PERIWINKLE

VINCA MAJOR

Although ebullient and easygoing, greater periwinkle is often passed over in favor of rarer plants. But its arching stems and cheerful blooms have great charm, and its ease of growth means it can be used in many ways, from pots to window boxes and hanging baskets, for year-round color.

PLANT TYPE Hardy, evergreen, herbaceous plant

HEIGHT 12 in (30 cm), trailing to 12 in (30 cm) in a pot

SPREAD Up to 18 in (45 cm) in a pot

POT SIZE One plant per 12 in- (30 cm-) diameter pot; three plants per 16 in- (40 cm-) diameter basket

CALENDAR

	WINTER		SPRING		SUMMER		FALL	
IN LEAF								
IN FLOWER								

COLOR

LEAVES Green

FLOWERS Violet-blue

Greater periwinkle will cascade from your window boxes and hanging baskets.

Variegated periwinkle 'Maculata' is as valuable for its leaves as for its flowers.

CHOOSE

This versatile plant is most often found with variegated leaves. 'Variegata' has leaves that are edged with pale yellow, fading to cream, 'Maculata' produces leaves with bright yellow centers, while 'Wojo's Jem' has pale yellow centers. The variety *Vinca major* var. *oxyloba* offers darker blue flowers.

The closely related species *V. minor* is smaller in all its parts but has a wider choice of cultivars, including the free-flowering 'Bowles's Variety' and the bright yellow variegated 'Illumination'.

PERFECT PARTNERS Variegated kinds mix well with plain green evergreens and spring bulbs. **LARGE** *Fatsia japonica*, *Salix integra* 'Hakuro-nishiki' **MEDIUM** *Euonymus, Phormium, Sarcococca* **SMALL** *Hosta, Liriope muscari, Narcissus*

PLANT

Periwinkles are often sold in small pots in the "ground-cover" section of garden centers, especially in spring or fall. Plant in any good potting mix and, for quick effect, put several small plants together in pots, or in window boxes and hanging baskets to trail over.

GROW

Moist soil and regular feeding are necessary for vigorous growth, which is the most attractive. Plants may suffer in the heat of summer, so a part-shaded spot is best. To show off the bright new growth, which carries the flowers, trim off all the old growth in early spring, unless needed to cascade from baskets, window boxes, troughs, or pots.

MAINTAIN Feed every spring as new growth is produced for maximum flowers and stem growth. After several years, plants may lose vigor as the base gets congested with old stems. Plants can be divided in spring and replanted, or shoots can be pegged to the soil where they will root.

Some plants look good whatever the weather. This grouping features evergreens for sun and shade as well as plants that just want to please, flowering for months on end.

FOR YEAR-ROUND INTEREST

There are several terrific, all-purpose plants that will inject sparkle and interest in your garden or patio when there are lulls in the display of bright and fleeting flowers. These plants will keep your outside spaces looking great all year.

MULTI-SEASON PLANTS

Container plants need not be for one season only—there are a few very special plants, such as perennial wallflowers, that seem never to be out of flower and shine for much of the year. Heathers peak in late summer, but their foliage is always colorful, especially if you choose cultivars with yellow and orange leaves, which can assume different shades as the seasons change. But few plants give better value than laurustinus (*Viburnum tinus*), which flowers through winter and spring, and also often in fall—the flower buds are decorative, too, a feature shared with *Skimmia japonica*, which you should make room for, no matter how small your patio.

WINTER FLOWERS

Include some plants for winter interest and you will be tempted outside, even in the coldest spells. Winter flowers tend to be small, but every bit of color is extra special in these long, cold months. The flowers of sweet box (*Sarcococca*) are tiny but exude a sweet perfume in cold weather, while daphnes, which smell even sweeter, have showy blooms—they are invaluable on a patio, where you can enjoy their beauty up close. Australian fuchsias (*Correa pulchella*) are special, and deserve a prominent place where their winter flowers can be fully appreciated; they have dainty foliage all year but excel in winter, with their masses of fabulous blooms.

TOP-VALUE EVERGREENS

Evergreens are especially beautiful in winter, when there are fewer flowers to compete for our attention. Forming neutral backgrounds for summer flowers, their structure and foliage really come to the fore at this time of year. Their leaves can be surprisingly diverse in color, shape, size, and texture, so combine as many as possible to keep your patio packed with year-round interest. Evergreens are the perfect choice if you have a shady site as many of them have evolved to grow where there is little sunlight; the glossy texture of sweet box and holly reflects light and brightens any dark areas.

SILVER SWORD *ASTELIA CHATHAMICA*

This plant's arching, metallic leaves make a statement in any grouping. Silver swords are long-lived and become large specimen plants over many years. Mature plants produce clusters of small flowers and, occasionally, orange berries. They are evergreen and thrive in sun or part shade.

PLANT TYPE Hardy, evergreen perennial; may need protection below 14°F (−10°C)
HEIGHT Up to 3 ft 3 in (1 m) in a pot
SPREAD Up to 3 ft 3 in (1 m) in a pot
POT SIZE One plant per 12 in- (30 cm-) diameter pot; needs a larger pot after a year

CALENDAR

	WINTER	SPRING	SUMMER	FALL
IN LEAF	▓	▓	▓	▓
IN FLOWER			▓	

COLOR
LEAVES Silvery green
FLOWERS Green

GROW

Keep plants moist at all times and feed them regularly with a liquid fertilizer every week from spring to summer. This is especially important when plants fill the container and the foliage covers and cascades from it, making it difficult to get water into the top of the pot. In summer, it helps to stand the pot in a saucer, but this must be removed by fall to avoid waterlogging.

MAINTAIN Remove any old leaves from the center of your silver swords to keep the plants looking neat. After several years, they can be cut into sections to divide them, preferably in spring. They withstand wind well and are ideal for seaside gardens, but extreme cold damages the foliage, so covering with fleece in cold periods will maintain their appearance.

CHOOSE

This plant is the most widely grown *Astelia*. It is sometimes sold as the cultivar 'Silver Sword', even though this is just the common name. Its leaves are green above and more silvery below.

The closely related species *A. nervosa* is a smaller plant, with narrower leaves that are often suffused with a metallic bronze sheen. 'Westland' has a bronze color that is more pronounced during the cold weather.

PERFECT PARTNERS Silver sword's eye-catching foliage looks good with grasses, large, architectural foliage, and pink, white, and blue flowers in summer. **LARGE** *Canna*, *Melianthus major*, *Olea europaea* **MEDIUM** *Correa pulchella*, *Euphorbia*, *Phormium* **SMALL** *Festuca glauca*, *Heliotropium arborescens*, *Liriope muscari*

PLANT

Silver swords are easy to grow and will live for many years as long as they have perfect drainage—they will not tolerate waterlogged conditions. Plant them in spring or summer, using lime-free potting mix. These plants are not lime haters but the porous nature of lime-free mixes suits them well. Silver swords can thrive in surprisingly small pots; in fall or winter do not put small plants in large pots as this would surround them with wet potting mix when they least need it.

Astelia nervosa is a striking specimen plant that deserves space to arch naturally.

Pull out old leaves of *A. chathamica* to keep your plants neat and silvery.

HEATHER *CALLUNA VULGARIS*

Heathers are invaluable for their year-round interest. Their flowers are small but profuse and a magnet for bees and other pollinators. The foliage is often yellow and turns bronze in cold weather. Heather is hardy and grows wild in exposed, sunny areas but will not thrive in shady conditions.

PLANT TYPE Hardy, evergreen shrub
HEIGHT Up to 12in (30cm) in a pot
SPREAD Up to 12in (30cm) in a pot
POT SIZE Three plants per 12in- (30cm-) diameter pot
☼

CALENDAR

	WINTER	SPRING	SUMMER	FALL
IN LEAF				
IN FLOWER				

COLOR

LEAVES Green, yellow, bronze, or orange
FLOWERS White, pink, crimson, or purple

GROW

Heathers do not have deep roots so shallow pots are suitable, providing plants are not allowed to dry out—water them regularly to prevent this. Feed weekly through spring and summer. Keep pots of heather in full sun at all times. The soil surface should be free from weeds in the first season until it is covered by the heather foliage.

MAINTAIN Heathers can become bare at the base with brown foliage. To prevent this, prune them every year. Trim off the flowered shoots in fall, or in spring before growth starts. Plants in baskets and pots can be left *in situ* for several years or removed and potted separately for replanting.

Heathers fill containers with easy-care, fluffy color for many months.

CHOOSE

The most popular heathers are the bud-blooming Garden Girls Series, which remain in bloom for many months: 'Anette' is pink, 'Alicia' is white, and 'Athene' is purple. They are often sold with different varieties in one pot. Winter-flowering heathers (*Erica carnea* and *E. × darleyensis*) are particularly useful for spring displays.

PERFECT PARTNERS Plant heather alone in pots or with wispy plants that will not crowd them. Underplant with spring bulbs when heathers are not in bloom. **LARGE** *Juniperus scopulorum* 'Sky Rocket', *Salix integra* 'Hakuro-nishiki' **MEDIUM** *Carex*, *Euphorbia*, *Lavandula* **SMALL** *Dianthus*, *Festuca glauca*, *Narcissus*

PLANT

Heathers can be planted at any time of the year, but they are most commonly sold in bloom in summer. One plant can spread widely in time, but for more immediate effect in pots, plant them with about 3 in (8 cm) between them so that they will fill in within a year or so. Callunas need lime-free soil so must be planted in lime-free potting mix. They may be combined with seasonal flowers in the first year after planting but these will not need to be replaced in the second year.

Being completely hardy, heathers will withstand both frost and snow.

AUSTRALIAN FUCHSIA

CORREA PULCHELLA

These evergreen shrubs have attractive foliage and pretty, bell-shaped flowers. They make mounds of elegant, rounded leaves, often with grayish or rusty undersides. Australian fuchsias are suitable for coastal gardens but may not flourish in cold inland and upland sites.

PLANT TYPE Half-hardy, evergreen shrub; wind-tolerant; may need protection below 23°F (−5°C)
HEIGHT 24–36 in (60–90 cm) in a pot
SPREAD 24–36 in (60–90 cm) in a pot
POT SIZE One plant per 12 in- (30 cm-) diameter pot
☼

CALENDAR

	WINTER	SPRING	SUMMER	FALL
IN LEAF	▓▓▓	▓▓▓	▓▓▓	▓▓▓
IN FLOWER	▓▓▓	▓		

COLOR

LEAVES Silver-gray, gray-green
FLOWERS Red, pink, or orange

In a sheltered spot, Australian fuchsia will enliven winter with its delicate blooms.

CHOOSE

Australian fuchsia has gorgeous red, pink, or orange flowers set against dainty, dark green leaves. It has a bushy, compact habit and blooms in winter, when few other plants are in flower. Although small, the flowers are freely produced and create a lovely show on a sheltered, sunny patio.

If you are in search of a more hardy species, try *Correa backhouseana*, which has brown-rimmed leaves and beige flowers for many months, but is not as compact as *C. pulchella*. Several hybrids are also available, including 'Marian's Marvel', which has pink and yellow bells.

PERFECT PARTNERS The grayish foliage and open habit of Australian fuchsias make them good companions for other sun-loving plants. **LARGE** *Olea europaea, Pseudopanax lessonii, Trachelospermum jasminoides* **MEDIUM** *Alstroemeria, Astelia chathamica, Phormium* **SMALL** *Lavandula, Osteospermum, Verbena* (trailing)

PLANT

Australian fuchsias are usually sold, in bloom, in winter and spring. They can be planted at any time of the year, but protect them from extreme cold and, if possible, place them in porches, against the house, or in some other protected spot. Young plants are more vulnerable to cold than mature plants.

Plant Australian fuchsias in enriched potting mix; they are very easily damaged by waterlogged soil, so it is always best to use terra-cotta or ceramic containers for porosity.

GROW

Water plants freely in spring and summer and keep them moist at all times, especially in winter. Feed with a high-potash fertilizer from spring to fall. Young plants may need staking at first, until they are established, especially in exposed situations.

MAINTAIN Prune your plants lightly in spring, removing most of the flowered growth: this will keep them compact and less likely to produce long, straggly stems. In fall, be prepared to protect them with fleece on cold nights, removing it in mild periods to display the flowers. Show off the plants in winter by moving them to sheltered areas by the house.

DAPHNE *DAPHNE ODORA*

This dome-shaped evergreen shrub is valued for its fragrant flowers that open in spring. Although not showy, they are impossible to ignore because they perfume the air around them. Many daphnes are tricky to please, but this plant is reliable in all but the coldest gardens.

PLANT TYPE Evergreen shrub; may need protection below 23°F (−5°C)
HEIGHT Up to 36 in (90 cm) in a pot
SPREAD 36 in (90 cm) in a pot
POT SIZE One plant per 12 in- (30 cm-) diameter pot

CALENDAR

	WINTER	SPRING	SUMMER	FALL
IN LEAF				
IN FLOWER				

COLOR

LEAVES Rich, lustrous green, sometimes variegated
FLOWERS White, from pink buds

GROW

Keep plants moist at all times. Growth occurs in a flush after flowering, so feed plants every week in late spring and summer—this is not essential in fall as the growth matures. A high-potash fertilizer to encourage flowering is best; but if the foliage has yellowed, due to a sunny site, a more balanced fertilizer, with more nitrogen, is beneficial. Turn the pot a few times throughout the year to encourage balanced growth.

MAINTAIN Daphne does not need regular pruning, but pinch out any long shoots in spring, soon after flowering, to help more shoots grow from the base. Most daphnes are intolerant of pruning, but *D. odora* and *D. bholua* can be lightly pruned; you can also cut small sprigs to enjoy their perfume indoors.

Daphne's delicate flowers fill the winter air with sweet perfume.

CHOOSE

In the springtime, *Daphne odora*'s flowers will be the highlight of your patio, unmistakable and unmissable with their glorious fragrance.

This reliable plant is most often sold as the subtly variegated cultivar 'Aureomarginata'. In recent years, more spectacularly variegated forms, such as 'Mae-jima', have become readily available and increasingly popular.

An alternative species to *D. odora* is *D. bholua*, which is taller and just as fragrant but not as easy to grow in a container as *D. odora*. PERFUME PRINCESS is a hybrid between these two species, with a profusion of magnificent pink, scented flowers.

PERFECT PARTNERS In summer, the glossy green leaves offer a backdrop to vibrant flowers and distinctive, large or linear foliage. **LARGE** *Fatsia japonica, Nerium oleander, Pseudopanax lessonii* **MEDIUM** *Astelia chathamica, Euphorbia, Lantana camara* **SMALL** *Helleborus, Nerine bowdenii, Yucca*

PLANT

Daphne grows well in sun or part shade and tolerates lime in the soil. It is slightly tender and flowers best in a sunny, sheltered position, though this can lead to sparse and yellowish foliage—if this happens, feeding with a nitrogen-rich fertilizer may help. Placing your pot in part shade will give lusher, greener leaves, but flowering will be reduced. Plant into enriched potting mix.

Reduce the length of long shoots by pinching them out in spring.

PINK *DIANTHUS*

These annual and perennial plants are loved for their fragrant blooms. At their peak in early summer, the traditional kinds flower once; more modern kinds do so throughout summer, but not all have strong scent. The blue-gray leaves of some are decorative in their own right.

PLANT TYPE Hardy perennial or half-hardy annual

HEIGHT Up to 6–18 in (15–45 cm) in a pot, depending on species

SPREAD Up to 8–12 in (20–30 cm) in a pot, depending on species

POT SIZE Three plants per 12 in- (30 cm-) diameter pot

CALENDAR

	WINTER	SPRING	SUMMER	FALL
IN LEAF				
IN FLOWER				

COLOR

LEAVES Green, gray-green, or silver

FLOWERS White, salmon-pink, rose-pink, red, lilac, or bicolored

Deadhead dianthus flowers for more and larger blooms and to keep plants tidy.

CHOOSE

Among the perennials, the Allwoodii Group of pinks (such as pink 'Doris') and the Devon pinks (such as purple 'Devon Wizard') bloom for months and have double flowers. The annual bedding pinks based on *Dianthus barbatus,* as in the Festival Series, have single flowers in a wide range of colors.

Annual pinks are attractive bedding plants that withstand light frosts.

PERFECT PARTNERS The annual pinks combine well with other summer bedding plants; the perennials mix with silver foliage and shrubby herbs such as lavender. **LARGE** *Cordyline australis, Olea europaea, Salix integra* 'Hakuro-nishiki' **MEDIUM** *Lavandula, Lilium, Penstemon* **SMALL** *Fuchsia, Heliotropium arborescens, Verbena*

PLANT

You can buy perennial dianthus plants in spring or summer—these will be frost hardy. The annuals are sold in late spring and will tolerate slight frosts, but these plants should be treated as half-hardy annuals. They will bloom into fall, until the first frosts, but their flowers tend to be damaged by damp, cold weather.

The annual kinds can be planted in any potting mix, but use an enriched potting mix for perennial pinks. Never crowd them with other plants. which may cause them to rot, and also avoid planting them deeper than they were in the pots in which you originally bought them.

GROW

Annual pinks should be watered and fed freely. Deadhead the old flowers to keep plants tidy and prevent dead blooms causing mold on foliage and stems. Perennials need full sun and air movement around them to prevent rot and must have well-drained potting mix. Feed them weekly from spring to late summer. Each stem produces several flowers and when the last of these fades, snap off the stem at the base.

MAINTAIN In early fall, when the plants stop flowering, pull up annual pinks. Perennial pinks will last for several years but are at their best in the first and second year. As they age they get straggly, with dead, brown stems at the base. It is possible to improve their appearance with a light prune in spring but plants need replacing after three years.

PERENNIAL WALLFLOWER *ERYSIMUM*

Magnets for butterflies, these shrubs bloom from spring to fall. Their flowers are showy, often scented, and colorful for longer than most plants. Some are fragrant, too, but it is for their showy display that they are valued most.

PLANT TYPE Hardy, evergreen shrub; needs protection below 23°F (–5°C)

HEIGHT Up to 16in (40cm) in a pot, depending on cultivar

SPREAD Up to 16in (40cm) in a pot

POT SIZE One plant per 12in- (30cm-) diameter pot

CALENDAR

	WINTER	SPRING	SUMMER	FALL
IN LEAF				
IN FLOWER				

COLOR

LEAVES Green or gray-green, sometimes variegated

FLOWERS Mauve, purple, red, yellow, or orange

'Red Jep' is a popular wallflower that blooms almost all year in a sunny spot.

CHOOSE

The perennial wallflower is valued most for its showy flowers, borne through much of the year; some are fragrant, too. Several cultivars are available; of these, the most popular is the reliable 'Bowles's Mauve', with its gorgeous mauve blooms. The smaller 'Red Jep' is stocky with fragrant, red flowers. Newer cultivars offer a wide range of colors and are hardy.

PERFECT PARTNERS Erysimums mix well with summer bedding plants and other sun-loving perennials, especially those with gray or silver foliage. **LARGE** *Laurus nobilis, Olea europaea, Salix integra* 'Hakuro-nishiki' **MEDIUM** *Euphorbia, Lavandula* **SMALL** *Festuca glauca, Nemesia*

PLANT

Plants are usually available as small plants in spring or mature plants in full flower in summer. These large, spreading plants will oust and smother smaller, slow-growers. If you want them for a year or less, plant in any good potting mix in a mixed pot of plants. If you want to keep plants for several years, grow them in their own pot with enriched potting mix, which will ensure slower growth and longer-lived plants.

GROW

Perennial wallflowers often live for two years before they get straggly and start to collapse under their own weight. This happens most rapidly if they are watered and fed excessively, so avoid over-feeding; grow in enriched potting mix in full sun. In shade they soon become straggly and do not flower well. Use high-potash fertilizer and feed fortnightly while plants are in bloom.

MAINTAIN Flowers appear on long stems from the shoot tips. When the last blooms fade, cut them off to keep plants tidy. Young plants respond well to pruning. Cut them back, if necessary, in spring or summer but not fall, as regrowth is prone to damage by frost. Replace plants after two years; cuttings taken from summer to early fall root readily. In cold areas, plants may need protection from fleece in winter.

'Bowles's Mauve' has grayish leaves and showy flowers on long spikes.

HOLLY *ILEX AQUIFOLIUM*

The common holly is a useful and popular evergreen for shade or sun. It can be grown as a free-form bush or pruned into cones or standards. With just one exception (the cultivar 'J.C. van Tol'), plants are either male or female: both are needed for the female to produce berries.

PLANT TYPE Hardy, evergreen shrub
HEIGHT Up to 6 ft 6 in (2 m) in a pot
SPREAD Up to 3 ft 3 in (1 m) in a pot
POT SIZE One plant per 12 in- (30 cm-) diameter pot
☼ ☼

CALENDAR

	WINTER	SPRING	SUMMER	FALL
IN LEAF				
IN FLOWER				

COLOR

LEAVES Green, variegated with yellow or white
FLOWERS White, small

If only lightly pruned, female hollies will produce bright berries in fall.

CHOOSE

If you are looking for a ready-trained holly, there will be little choice of cultivar. Variegated hollies are the most popular. 'Handsworth New Silver' has boldly white-edged leaves and fruits well. 'Golden Milkboy' is male and has yellow-blotched leaves. The hybrid *Ilex* × *altaclerensis* has almost spineless leaves. The variegated 'Lawsoniana' and 'Golden King' (both female) are widely grown. Female hollies produce berries that ripen in fall and last into winter. 'J.C. van Tol' is unusual for being self-fertile. Both the flowers and berries of a holly plant attract wildlife to the garden.

PERFECT PARTNERS The glossy foliage contrasts well with darker leaves. Variegated hollies complement yellow and white flowers. **LARGE** *Fatsia japonica, Hedera colchica, Phyllostachys nigra* **MEDIUM** *Buxus sempervirens, Hemerocallis, Lilium* **SMALL** *Begonia, Heuchera, Hosta*

PLANT

Plant hollies at any time with enriched potting mix. These are long-lived plants, so use good potting mix and repot, as necessary, every few years as they grow. Standard plants will need support at all times. If you want berries, you must plant both male and female hollies: only the females will produce berries and one male will fertilize several female plants, if grown in close proximity.

GROW

Keep plants moist at all times. Hollies do not wilt if the soil is dry but will react by dropping foliage weeks later. Feed weekly in spring and summer. Some leaf drop is natural in late spring as the new foliage is maturing. Pinch back growing tips while they are still soft, in early summer, reducing them by half their length, to maintain dense growth.

MAINTAIN If overgrown, hollies can be pruned hard in spring. This is useful if they have been neglected and become straggly. These plants are prone to attack by scale insects (see p.37), especially if neglected. This is usually first spotted by the appearance of black mold on the leaves. Hollies are also attacked by the leaf miner insect, which creates brown blotches in the leaves. Regular watering and feeding reduces the impact of both these problems.

A clipped, standard holly is a feature all year and contrasts with bright violas.

SWEET BOX *SARCOCOCCA*

The glossy leaves of sarcococcas are attractive all year, but most useful in winter. Although able to survive even dense shade, their main attraction is their flowers, which open in winter—these are insignificant but highly fragrant. Blooms are followed by red or black berries, held below the foliage.

PLANT TYPE Hardy, evergreen shrub; needs protection from direct sunlight

HEIGHT 36 in (90 cm) in a pot, depending on species

SPREAD 24 in (60 cm), in a pot, depending on species

POT SIZE One plant per 12 in- (30 cm-) diameter pot

☀ ☀

CALENDAR

COLOR

LEAVES Dark green
FLOWERS Small, white

	WINTER		SPRING		SUMMER		FALL	
IN LEAF								
IN FLOWER								

Young plants are slender and elegant but bush out and thicken as they grow.

A small sweet box (middle row) adds fragrance to a winter display.

CHOOSE

Sturdy and generally easy to grow, this dense, winter-flowering, shade-loving shrub is adored for the wonderful fragrance of its tiny, white flowers.

All species of *Sarcococca* are very much alike: *S. confusa* has black berries, while *S. ruscifolia* has red berries, but is otherwise similar; *S. hookeriana* is more upright in habit, with purple stems. WINTER GEM is a recent, compact hybrid, ideal for containers, with berries that ripen from red to black. All these plants are hardy and at their very best when they are protected from intense and direct sunlight.

PERFECT PARTNERS The upright stems are clothed with fine-textured leaves that are not spectacular in themselves but a useful foil for other shade-loving plants. **LARGE** *Camellia, Fatsia japonica, Phyllostachys nigra, Viburnum tinus* **MEDIUM** *Dryopteris erythrosora, Euonymus fortunei* **SMALL** *Begonia, Hosta, Liriope muscari*

PLANT

Plant your sweet box in enriched potting mix. Small plants can be surrounded by temporary bedding plants for the first year, but these plants create dense shade, which will make underplanting difficult in later years. They produce new stems from near ground level, creating a multi-stemmed plant that gets thicker each year.

GROW

Sweet box are easy to please and withstand some neglect, though this will lead to leaf loss. They do not tolerate waterlogging, so never stand their pots in saucers. Keep plants evenly moist and feed once a week with liquid fertilizer from spring to late summer, when new growth is being produced.

MAINTAIN As plants mature they develop taller stems. If these are too tall for your liking, trim them at the end of summer. Old stems become very twiggy and lose leaves after several years—these can be pruned out at ground level at any time. When it is not possible to repot into larger pots, plants will survive in surprisingly small pots, as long as they are fed regularly. If foliage becomes yellow, it is usually due to lack of nutrients or the fact that the plant would benefit from more shade.

SKIMMIA *SKIMMIA JAPONICA*

These are popular plants for fall containers because of their long-lasting, showy flower buds. Their foliage is neat and the flowers, which open in spring, are sweetly scented. Female skimmias produce showy berries, too, so these lovely plants have many seasons of interest.

PLANT TYPE Hardy, evergreen shrub
HEIGHT Up to 30in (75cm) in a pot
SPREAD Up to 30in (75cm) in a pot
POT SIZE One plant per 12in- (30cm-) diameter pot

CALENDAR

	WINTER			SPRING			SUMMER			FALL		
IN LEAF	■	■	■	■	■	■	■	■	■	■	■	■
IN FLOWER				■	■							

COLOR

LEAVES Mid-green
FLOWERS Cream

CHOOSE

By far the most popular and widely grown skimmia is 'Rubella', which is male and has large, compact heads of red buds in fall and winter. Variegated forms have recently been introduced, which have gray-flushed leaves with cream edges. 'Magic Marlot', 'Perosa', 'Nymans', and the more compact Obsession are all good choices if you want berries—but both male and female plants are needed for the female to produce these.

The vibrant flower buds of 'Rubella' are usually unharmed by frost.

PERFECT PARTNERS Skimmia's rounded, mid-green leaves contrast with strap-like and larger leaves. The spring flowers give fragrance to accent colorful spring bedding. **LARGE** *Fatsia japonica, Musa basjoo, Trachycarpus fortunei* **MEDIUM**, *Euonymus fortunei, Lilium, Pseudopanax lessonii* **SMALL** *Hakonechloa macra, Helleborus, Hosta*

PLANT

Skimmias are often sold as small plants in fall, with flower clusters present, for window boxes and pots. Larger plants are available, and can be planted, all year. Skimmias need lime-free soil, so plant them in a potting mix intended for acid loving plants. In soil containing lime, the foliage turns yellow and growth is always poor. In their first season, small plants can be surrounded by seasonal bedding but, as they grow and spread the shade they produce will prevent underplanting.

GROW

Skimmias require well-drained soil and dislike waterlogging. Keep the potting mix moist and feed every week from spring to late summer. An ericaceous fertilizer is an advantage. Remove old flower clusters from male skimmias in early summer to keep plants neat. Skimmias grow naturally as neat domes but can be pruned in spring to give them shape.

MAINTAIN These plants need little attention but unless fed sufficiently or repotted it is common for them to lose vigor—new growth becomes shorter and leaves pale green. To prevent this, top-dress plants every year with time-release fertilizer. Repot as appropriate.

Prune mature plants in spring to encourage new growth from the base.

LAURUSTINUS *VIBURNUM TINUS*

This tough and reliable shrub is notable for the red flower buds that form in fall and open into white flowers throughout winter and spring. There are many cultivars but all, except the variegated forms, are similar with slight variations in habit and flowers.

PLANT TYPE Hardy, evergreen shrub
HEIGHT Up to 4 ft 9 in (1.5 m) in a pot
SPREAD Up to 3 ft 3 in (1 m) in a pot
POT SIZE One plant per 12 in- (30 cm-) diameter pot
☼ ◐

CALENDAR

	WINTER	SPRING	SUMMER	FALL
IN LEAF	▓	▓	▓	▓
IN FLOWER	▓	▓		▓

COLOR
LEAVES Deep green
FLOWERS White or pink

'Gwenllian' will produce a crop of purple-blue berries in springtime.

GROW

This viburnum is often planted in shade but will be more compact and will flower more freely in sun. Keep plants moist at all times and feed weekly from spring to fall. As they grow, the mounded bush spreads, which makes underplanting difficult. The production of berries is dependent on the weather when the flowers open, usually in spring. The flowers are damaged by frost but the buds will survive to open later when the weather improves.

MAINTAIN The growth of your laurustinus will be dictated by the amount of water and fertilizer it is given. In shaded positions, these plants are prone to become straggly, but this can be corrected by pruning in spring. If necessary, this can be quite severe; although flowering will be sparse in the year following pruning, the plant will be greatly improved.

Laurustinus provides structure all year and flowers in winter and spring.

CHOOSE

Laurustinus is a highly adaptable and readily available shrub that thrives in sun or part shade. Because this is a common hedging plant, keep a look out for named cultivars that are more compact and will give better value in a container. 'Eve Price' is an excellent choice, with small leaves and pink buds opening to white flowers. 'Gwenllian' is larger and has clusters of flowers tinged with pink. 'Lisarose' has pink flowers and Spirit flowers prolifically for longer than most. 'Variegatum' has leaves boldly splashed with primrose yellow. All these plants produce purple to black berries in fall. (See also *Viburnum davidii*, p.114.)

PERFECT PARTNERS The dark green leaves of laurustinus are rather somber but make an effective background for brighter flowers and foliage. **LARGE** *Fatsia japonica, Ficus carica, Olea europaea* **MEDIUM** *Choisya, Euonymus fortunei, Phormium* **SMALL** *Hosta, Liriope muscari, Vinca major*

PLANT

Plants are available all year. Small plants can be added to window boxes and even hanging baskets for winter display to be replaced in spring. Otherwise, plant your laurustinus in pots with enriched potting mix.

Pelargoniums are just some of the colorful and aromatic plants that can be relied on to flourish in sunny and exposed sites at ground level, on balconies, or in roof gardens.

FOR HOT SPOTS AND ROOFTOPS

Everyone loves a sunny patio or roof garden, where you can sit back, relax, and entertain friends and family—but they can be tough environments for plants. Happily, some of the most desirable container plants thrive in these harsh areas.

GROWING IN THE SUN

Some plants relish the sun and its warmth just as much as you do on a summer's day—silver-leaved plants, for example, have built-in sun-protection as their leaves reflect excess light. It can be tricky to keep plants constantly moist in summer, but these tough survivors will tolerate a little neglect. You can help keep your plants moist by planting them in glazed pots, which retain more moisture than stone or terra-cotta. Use organically enriched potting mixes because they absorb water better when rewetted after drying out. Large pots, when filled, will not get as hot as small pots—nor will they dry out as quickly, or blow over in windy weather.

CLASSIC CONTAINER PLANTS

Many of the most desirable plants thrive on a sun-baked patio. Who doesn't love a large container of sky-blue agapanthus, its huge globes of blooms towering above bold, strappy leaves? And this is also the place for palms, including the tough but striking, boldly architectural European fan palm (*Chamaerops humilis*). But the perfect plants for these sites—providing an unrivaled and lengthy display of color—are pelargoniums. Content in small pots and often flowering prolifically, even with treatment that would kill other plants, their showy flowers are a highlight all summer long. Everyone is familiar with their bright red flowers, but they are surprisingly diverse and will satisfy the need for pastel color as well as vibrant displays.

SCENT IN YOUR GARDEN

Your patio or roof garden is where you are closest to your plants for the longest time and also where you entertain friends and family. Scent can add a further dimension to your enjoyment of these spaces, and many of the plants that thrive in hot and windy conditions have aromatic foliage. Lavender is a great choice for patios, as are the easy-to-grow, scented-leaf pelargoniums, with aromas ranging from floral to citrus. Place your scented plants close to seating areas and wherever you may rub against them to release their perfume.

AFRICAN LILY *AGAPANTHUS*

Few plants are as imposing as African lilies in bloom—great globes of magnificent blue flowers above their glossy, strap-like leaves. They can be shy to bloom in the garden but will thrive and flower freely in pots, especially in full sun, when they will be the highlight of your summer garden.

PLANT TYPE Hardy, herbaceous perennial; some are evergreen; some need protection below 23°F (−5°C)

HEIGHT Up to 2–4 ft (60 cm–1.2 m) in a pot

SPREAD Up to 18 in–3 ft 3 in (45 cm–1 m)

POT SIZE One plant per 12 in- (30 cm-) diameter pot

CALENDAR

	WINTER		SPRING		SUMMER		FALL	
IN LEAF								
IN FLOWER								

COLOR

LEAVES Green

FLOWERS Blue, purple, or white

Dwarf African lilies are a good choice for window boxes in a sunny site.

CHOOSE

African lilies vary in hardiness but those that are deciduous, with narrow leaves, tolerate more cold than those with broad, evergreen foliage. 'Black Pantha', 'Purple Cloud', and 'Northern Star' have blue flowers and are deciduous. Queen Mum and Twister have blue and white flowers and are evergreen in mild areas.

PERFECT PARTNERS African lilies epitomize hot, summer days and look especially good with tropical foliage and flowers and plants that evoke the warmth and color of the Riviera. **LARGE** *Canna, Nerium oleander, Olea europaea* **MEDIUM** *Chamaerops, Euphorbia, Melianthus* **SMALL** *Alstroemeria, Heliotropium arborescens, Pelargonium*

PLANT

Buy African lilies as mature plants in spring or summer. They dislike root disturbance and take several years to establish from bare roots or small divisions. Pot into enriched potting mix. These are long-lived plants and have extensive, fleshy roots. Protect evergreen plants from frost in their first spring after planting until they build up some strength.

GROW

African lilies need a sunny position and thrive in a mild spot, sheltered from extreme cold. These plants can survive drought but grow and flower best when well fed and watered. Feed with high-potash fertilizer once a week from late spring to late summer.

Repot African lilies when the roots fill the original pot; if left too long, the roots may push the plant out of the pot. Flowering is most profuse when plants fill the pot with roots, but it will be reduced if they are overcrowded.

MAINTAIN Remove dead flower stems when the last flowers drop. Deciduous kinds are often hardy, but benefit from moving to a sheltered spot for winter to stop roots freezing. Evergreens will be damaged, but not always killed, if badly frosted and the potting mix freezes. Lining pots with bubble wrap (see p.33) is beneficial; wooden tubs can also help insulate and protect plants. African lilies can be covered in fleece for cold periods or moved to a greenhouse.

The distinctive African-lily blooms are long-lasting and great for pollinators.

EUROPEAN FAN PALM

CHAMAEROPS HUMILIS

This plant thrives in a sunny spot, withstands wind and drought, and is the second-hardiest palm, after *Trachycarpus*. Slow-growing, with age it produces side shoots at the base that make a handsome dome of tough, fan-shaped leaves. The foliage is usually gray-green but some is silvery.

PLANT TYPE Hardy, evergreen shrub
HEIGHT Up to 4 ft (1.2 m) in a pot
SPREAD Up to 4 ft (1.2 m) in a pot
POT SIZE One plant per 12 in- (30 cm-) diameter pot

CALENDAR

	WINTER	SPRING	SUMMER	FALL
IN LEAF	▓▓	▓▓	▓▓	▓▓
IN FLOWER			▓▓	

COLOR

LEAVES Gray-green, silvery
FLOWERS Cream, small, in large clusters

Their Mediterranean origin makes these plants ideal for terra-cotta pots.

CHOOSE

The bushy, medium-size palm *Chamaerops humilis* is the only European palm and the only species of this genus. It has a mass of striking, gray-green leaves with spiny stalks. If you are looking for a smaller plant, 'Vulcano' is the best choice; it is more compact and has fewer spines. *C. humilis* var. *cerifera* is notable for the bluish color of the leaves and it is also a compact plant. However, it needs a warm spot to thrive and is intolerant of winter wet.

PERFECT PARTNERS The dramatic appearance of this palm naturally suits other Mediterranean plants and those with striking foliage. **LARGE** *Cordyline australis, Nerium, Olea europaea* **MEDIUM** *Agapanthus, Euphorbia, Phormium* **SMALL** *Correa, Osteospermum, Yucca*

PLANT

This plant is slow-growing and tough. Large plants are very expensive, so most are bought as immature plants in 8 in (20 cm) pots. Pot these into 12 in (30 cm) pots in potting mix labeled for palms and keep them in a sunny position. They are best in their own container rather than mixed with other plants because of their slow growth.

Mature plants make a bold statement on a warm and sunny patio.

GROW

Keep European fan palms moist in spring and summer and feed every two weeks with general fertilizer. In winter, they should be just moist; avoid waterlogging. Stand your plants on pot feet to ensure good drainage.

MAINTAIN Cut off any old or brown leaves to keep plants neat. After several years, the palm will need to be moved into a larger pot, but avoid overpotting into large pots. Repot in spring so the plant can fill the new potting mix with roots before winter. In cold districts, it is best to move plants of *C. humilis* var. *cerifera* to a cold greenhouse or against the house to protect them.

MEXICAN ORANGE BLOSSOM *CHOISYA*

PLANT TYPE Hardy, evergreen shrub
HEIGHT Up to 30 in (75 cm) in a pot, depending on species
SPREAD Up to 30 in (75 cm) in a pot, depending on species
POT SIZE One plant per 12 in- (30 cm-) diameter pot
☀ ☀

Mexican orange blossoms are a long-standing favorite in gardens for their aromatic, glossy foliage and fragrant flowers. Adaptable to a range of conditions, they are great as small plants and as standout specimens in large pots.

CALENDAR

	WINTER	SPRING	SUMMER	FALL
IN LEAF				
IN FLOWER				

COLOR

LEAVES Glossy green or yellow
FLOWERS White

SUNDANCE is often planted in fall baskets as a temporary filler.

'Aztec Pearl' is grown for its finely divided leaves and fragrant flowers.

CHOOSE

This plant's dense, lustrous foliage is attractive all year. Recent developments have widened the appeal of choisyas, with a greater variety of foliage and flowers being introduced.

The common *Choisya ternata* is a vigorous, bushy shrub with glossy leaves. SUNDANCE is popular for its yellow leaves, while finely divided foliage is the main attraction of *C. × dewitteana* 'Aztec Pearl' and the yellow-leaved 'Aztec Gold'. WHITE DAZZLER is grown for its abundant flowers. All these plants flower in spring and summer (often in late summer).

PERFECT PARTNERS Choisyas combine well with plants of upright habit and bold foliage. **LARGE** *Canna, Juniperus scopulorum* 'Skyrocket', *Phyllostachys* **MEDIUM** *Ensete ventricosum, Lilium, Phormium* **SMALL** *Carex, Hosta, Yucca*

PLANT

Mexican orange blossoms are sold all year, either as small plants for window boxes in fall or as large shrubs. Small plants can be planted in mixed pots for temporary effect in winter and then removed in spring. If you are planting for permanent display, any good quality potting mix is suitable. Choisyas can be placed in sun or part shade, but they flower best in full sun.

GROW

Keep plants moist at all times and feed once a week from late spring to fall. They grow rapidly and can become spindly, especially in part shade. To maintain compact growth, pinch out the growing tips regularly. Turn the pot to maintain even growth. When the flowers fade, trim off the old flower clusters, along with a pair of leaves to encourage new, neat growth.

MAINTAIN Winter can take its toll on choisyas, scorching the soft shoot tips. Trim these off in spring, after the frosts. Avoid pruning too hard in spring or you may remove potential flower buds that would open in early summer. Plants can be pruned hard in spring if foliage is the main reason for growing them, being followed by a flush of vigorous leaves.

LAVENDER *LAVANDULA*

These plants are universally popular for their wonderful fragrance and colorful flowers—in full bloom, they buzz with bees and butterflies. Lavenders vary in size, color, and scent. Traditional kinds have outstanding fragrance, with flower heads that are suitable for cutting and drying.

PLANT TYPE Hardy, evergreen shrub
HEIGHT 12–18 in (30–45 cm) in a pot
SPREAD 12–18 in (30–45 cm) in a pot
POT SIZE One plant per 12 in- (30 cm-) diameter pot

CALENDAR

COLOR

LEAVES Gray or green
FLOWERS Lavender, purple, white, or blue

	WINTER	SPRING	SUMMER	FALL
IN LEAF				
IN FLOWER				

Traditional lavender brings fragrance to a patio and hums with bees in summer.

French lavender has attractive, showy flower heads but may not survive winter.

CHOOSE

Some of the best-scented lavenders are forms of *Lavandula angustifolia*, which have gray leaves and showy blooms; the rich blue 'Hidcote' and pale blue 'Munstead' are popular and compact. The French lavenders, hybrids of *L. stoechas*, have small flowers but showy tufts of bracts at the top of the flower heads. They are less hardy, need perfect drainage to thrive, and are not as sweetly scented as *L. angustifolia*.

PERFECT PARTNERS Lavender's gray foliage contrasts with other sun-loving shrubs. **LARGE** *Chamaerops humilis*, *Juniperus scopulorum* 'Skyrocket', *Olea europaea* **MEDIUM** *Correa* **SMALL** *Festuca glauca*, *Nerine bowdenii*, *Verbena*

PLANT

Lavenders are plants that originate from a dry, rocky terrain and so they do not thrive in moist, humus-rich soil. Pot them into enriched potting mix—the best time to do this is in spring or early summer so that they can establish before winter.

These plants can be potted with a mix of other similar plants but do not let them swamp the lavender. When shaded by other foliage, lavenders will die. They grow best in their own container, but different kinds can be grouped together. French lavenders are often treated as temporary plants and replaced each spring.

GROW

Keep plants moist and feed every two weeks from spring to late summer. Prune in spring and then again after flowering to remove the spent flowers along with some of the new growth.

MAINTAIN Most lavenders are hardy but French lavenders can succumb to wet winters: it is a mix of wet and cold that kills them, so it is a good idea to place them close to buildings for shelter. They are prone to rot, so avoid covering them with fleece for winter protection.

Lavenders grow quickly and should be pruned lightly twice a year. If left unpruned, they will get straggly and lose their lower foliage. If they are cut back into bare, leafless stems, they rarely regrow and the plants may die.

NERINE *NERINE BOWDENII*

These spectacular bulbs flower from mid to late fall, providing a last splash of vibrant color before winter. Their summer foliage is unassuming but more than compensated for by the unique flowers. Nerines thrive in containers and look better every year as the bulbs become crowded.

PLANT TYPE Hardy bulb; may need protection below 23°F (−5°C)

HEIGHT Up to 18 in (45 cm) in a pot

SPREAD Up to 4 in (10 cm) in a pot

POT SIZE Eight bulbs per 12 in- (30 cm-) diameter pot

☼

CALENDAR

COLOR

LEAVES Green

FLOWERS Pink, white

	WINTER	SPRING	SUMMER	FALL
IN LEAF				
IN FLOWER				

CHOOSE

This plant, with its vibrant pink flowers, is the only reliably hardy species of *Nerine*. Other forms of the species vary slightly in color. 'Lipstick', for example, has white flowers with pink tips and 'Ostara' and 'Vesta K' are the palest pink. 'Isabel' and 'Mr. John' both have dramatic, dark pink blooms.

This plant's brilliant pink flowers bloom surprisingly late in fall.

PERFECT PARTNERS Nerines look striking when placed behind low, sun-loving plants or in front of plain foliage. **LARGE** *Cordyline australis, Nerium oleander, Olea europaea* **MEDIUM** *Dahlia, Penstemon* **SMALL** *Festuca glauca, Heliotropium arborescens, Heuchera*

PLANT

Nerines are sold as potted bulbs in summer and fall and as dry bulbs in spring—plant both types in enriched potting mix. They flower only when established and when the bulbs are crowded, so bare-root bulbs may not flower freely in the first fall. They will produce foliage in summer.

Plant nerines with a gap of about 1 in (3 cm) between the bulbs and with the upper half of the bulb above the surface. You can cover the surface with gravel, if desired.

GROW

Keep plants moist all year and feed with a liquid fertilizer in spring and summer, while they are in leaf. When the leaves

die back in fall, trim them away to tidy the pot and show off the flowers. The blooms last a month or so and, when they fade, the stems should be cut off at the base. Plants are dormant in winter and can then be placed somewhere under cover away from extreme cold. Pots can be allowed to get dry, but not for prolonged periods.

MAINTAIN When the bulbs fill their pot, repot them into a larger container, preferably in springtime. Divide the clump into three and space them out in their new pot to give them more room. After several years, the bulbs can get so crowded that they push themselves out of the pot—if this happens, you can divide and replant them in fresh potting mix.

If necessary, after several years, nerines can be divided in late summer or spring.

OLEANDER *NERIUM OLEANDER*

These hugely popular patio plants flower all summer and into fall, with blooms that come in a variety of colors. Their dark green foliage is attractive throughout the year. Although not reliably hardy, oleanders will survive harsh conditions, especially on bright, dry patios.

PLANT TYPE Evergreen shrub; needs protection below 32°F (0°C)
HEIGHT 4 ft 9 in (1.5 m) in a pot
SPREAD 30 in (75 cm) in a pot
POT SIZE One plant per 12 in- (30 cm-) diameter pot
☼

CALENDAR

	WINTER		SPRING		SUMMER		FALL	
IN LEAF								
IN FLOWER								

COLOR

LEAVES Dark green
FLOWERS Pink, red, white, or pale yellow

Oleander flowers best in a sunny, warm spot—next to a wall is often ideal.

CHOOSE

Oleanders are widely available but are most often sold by color rather than cultivar name. The most common color is the single-flowered pink, but white, dark pink, salmon-pink, and pale yellow are also sold. Double-flowered oleanders have larger blooms, though sometimes they will only open fully in hot weather. Some plants have variegated leaves, streaked with pale yellow, but they do not flower as freely.

PERFECT PARTNERS The striking appearance of oleanders suits other tropical plants as well as summer bedding plants. **LARGE** *Canna, Ficus carica, Musa basjoo* **MEDIUM** *Agapanthus, Dahlia, Melianthus major* **SMALL** *Osteospermum, Penstemon, Petunia*

PLANT

Oleanders can be bought as small plants and as small, trained standards. They are usually available in spring and summer, and are best grown as specimens in their own containers, potted in enriched potting mix. You can place small bedding plants around the base of the plants in the first year, but as plants mature the potting mix usually gets too full of roots to allow this.

GROW

To produce the best flowers, keep your plants in a sunny spot. Make sure they are moist and feed them every week from late spring to fall. Oleanders will survive dry conditions but grow and flower better when well fed. Flowers can be reluctant to open in cool conditions. Encourage them to bloom by removing the three shoots that appear just below the flower clusters.

Prune your oleanders in spring, but take care with this task as the sap and all other parts of the plants are toxic. Wear gloves when handling—or wash your hands immediately after contact.

Always wear gloves when handling oleander as the plant is poisonous.

MAINTAIN Oleanders can survive outside in mild areas. Covering with fleece in the coldest periods will keep the worst frosts off them. They survive best if the potting mix is fairly dry, but do not allow them to remain dry for long periods. These plants are best kept in a greenhouse or porch over winter, but they usually survive outside, especially in warm, urban, and seaside areas.

GERANIUM *PELARGONIUM*

Pelargoniums vary in size, color, and use, but all of them love sunshine. They are one of the most tolerant plants for pots, surviving spells of drought. Although adored for the vivid red of the common kinds, there is enough variety and plenty of pastels to create subtle, sophisticated displays.

PLANT TYPE Half-hardy perennial; needs protection below 41°F (5°C)

HEIGHT 8–18 in (20–45 cm) in a pot, some trailing to 12 in (30 cm)

SPREAD Up to 12 in (30 cm) in a pot

POT SIZE One to three plants per 12 in- (30 cm-) diameter pot

☼

CALENDAR

	WINTER	SPRING	SUMMER	FALL
IN LEAF				
IN FLOWER				

COLOR

LEAVES Green, often with a bronze ring; sometimes yellow or variegated

FLOWERS White, pink, red, or mauve

The Unique group of plants has large flowers and fragrant leaves, while Regal pelargoniums have the most spectacular flowers, larger than any other type, but they need a spot out of strong winds and have a quite short flowering period.

PERFECT PARTNERS

Red pelargoniums are terrific partners for other summer bedding plants. But the plant's fabulous range of colors allows for more creative combinations, and scented-leaf and trailing ivy-leaved kinds provide a wealth of planting combinations. **LARGE** *Cordyline australis, Laurus nobilis, Olea europaea* **MEDIUM** *Alstroemeria, Hemerocallis, Penstemon* **SMALL** *Calibrachoa, Dianthus, Heliotropium arborescens*

CHOOSE

The most popular pelargoniums are Zonal pelargoniums, which have clusters of flowers and foliage marked with a bronze ring. They are usually grown from seed, bred for a bushy habit, and free-flowering. Most have single flowers with five petals and are discarded at the end of fall.

Modern hybrids perform better. Raised from cuttings, they include a number of plants with double flowers and compact growth. The color range is vast and includes bicolors. Many of the older cultivars have attractively patterned leaves that make a wonderful show, even when not in bloom.

Ivy-leaved pelargoniums are equally popular: with their waxy leaves and straggly habit, they are perfect for hanging baskets and trailing over the edge of pots. These plants are usually grown from cuttings. The double-flowered kinds are often compact plants, but the small-flowered Balcon group, with slender growth, are particularly popular for window boxes.

Less common, but invaluable in any garden or patio, are scented-leaf pelargoniums. This group varies hugely in habit and many of them have attractive foliage and blooms, although most are small-flowered. These pelargoniums offer a wonderful range of fragrances, including rose, lemon, nutmeg, and apple. Most are extremely robust growers and suitable for less than ideal conditions.

Red pelargoniums are traditional and much-loved pot plants for sunny patios.

With its violet-blue flowers, BLUE SYBIL is vibrant in any context.

PLANT

Plant pelargoniums in spring, when all danger of frost has passed. They are usually available as small plants in pots, but seed-raised plants may be sold in cell packs. These plants suffer from gray mold, which will spread rapidly through the foliage if plants are crowded and the foliage is wet, so always check the young plants if they are being sold close together in displays.

If you are growing pelargoniums for a single summer or planting them with other plants, use commercial potting mix and give them room to grow: allow at least 4 in (10 cm) between each plant, more if planting early in the summer.

However, if you are growing plants that you want to keep longer than one year, or pelargoniums grouped together in the same pot (not mixed with other plants), use enriched potting mix, which will suit them better.

Regal pelargoniums have large blooms that can be damaged by rain, which makes them great for window boxes and sheltered patios.

GROW

Keep plants moist, not wet. Do not apply too much general fertilizer as this can lead to vigorous growth at the expense of flowers. Tomato fertilizer or other high-potash fertilizer suits them as it promotes flowers, not foliage. This is also relevant to those grown for their colored foliage. If plants grow too tall and do not branch well, pinch out the tips for bushiness. This does not apply to modern kinds, bred to be bushy, but it is useful for scented-leaf types.

Remove old flowers as they fade. If petals are allowed to drop onto lower leaves they can cause rot on the leaves. Double-flowered kinds can rot in wet weather and should also be removed to keep plants neat. Not all kinds will set seed but deadheading is advisable, snapping off the flower stems at the base.

MAINTAIN Pelargoniums may survive winters outside in mild or coastal areas but generally they must be protected from frost. The simplest way is to dig them out of their pot before the first frost in late summer and let them dry out. Do not prune them but allow the leaves to drop off. Keep them in an open cardboard box so air can circulate around them and store in a light, frost-free place. Some will survive this and can be cut back and repotted in spring.

Pots of pelargoniums can be stored more successfully in a cold greenhouse. Keep pots of plants almost dry. Many leaves will drop but the plants will survive if kept in an airy and dry environment. An even more certain way to keep them is to take cuttings in early fall. They root readily and the small plants can be kept on a windowsill in a light, cool room.

Scented-leaf pelargoniums offer a range of smells, and some repel insects.

Repot overwintered plants in spring. Feed them when new growth appears.

HOUSELEEK *SEMPERVIVUM*

These hardy succulents can survive with minimal care and are often seen on walls and the roofs of old cottages. There is huge variety in the size and color of houseleek rosettes, which are surprisingly colorful. When mature, these rosettes produce short stems of pink or red flowers.

PLANT TYPE Hardy, evergreen perennial
HEIGHT 2–8 in (5–20 cm) in flower in a pot
SPREAD 12 in (30 cm) in a pot
POT SIZE Three to five plants per 12 in- (30 cm-) diameter pot

CALENDAR

	WINTER	SPRING	SUMMER	FALL
IN LEAF				
IN FLOWER				

COLOR

LEAVES Green, red, orange, bronze
FLOWERS Pink or red

Resistant to drought, houseleeks are perfect for vertical gardens.

CHOOSE

Houseleeks are tolerant of the type of neglect that would spell disaster for many plants. Most are forms or hybrids of *Sempervivum tectorum*. They develop rosettes about 3 in (8 cm) across when mature, with leaves that are typically green, marked with red at the tips or base. They produce their best color when grown in sun and kept rather dry. *S. arachnoideum* has small rosettes, tinged with red and covered in white webbing across the whole plant.

PERFECT PARTNERS Use houseleeks at the front of plant groups, with other sun lovers. **LARGE** *Cordyline australis, Nerium oleander, Olea europaea* **MEDIUM** *Aeonium arboreum, Correa, Erysimum* **SMALL** *Dianthus, Festuca glauca, Nerine bowdenii*

PLANT

Because houseleeks produce offsets freely, they are best planted as young plants. If you buy a large pot, it is usually easy to pull the clumps apart and plant small clusters 2 in (5 cm) apart. Use enriched potting mix. These plants do not have deep roots, so shallow pots or troughs are best. If using deep pots, fill the bottom half with gravel so the potting mix above is never wet. They can be planted at any time, but spring and summer are best. Watch out for birds in search of vine-weevil grubs (*see right*).

GROW

Keep houseleeks moist and feed once a month in summer. As plants grow, mature rosettes produce flower stems, and when these die the whole rosette should be cut or pulled out— the surrounding young rosettes will soon fill in the gap. Houseleeks are fully hardy and do not need special protection in winter, though poor drainage will damage the roots.

MAINTAIN Houseleeks can survive neglect and irregular watering, which may even enhance the color of their rosettes. Their main pest is vine-weevil grubs (*see p.36*), which regularly eat the roots, causing the rosettes to fall out of the potting mix. Care may be needed with recent plantings to protect the young plants against birds, which may pull them up, often when they are in search of grubs.

In summer, mature rosettes produce long stems with intriguing flowers.

SPANISH DAGGER *YUCCA*

Dramatic plants with spiky leaves, yuccas thrive in warm, sunny spots and tolerate some drought when mature. Large plants produce tall stems of creamy, bell-shaped flowers in summer. Plants vary in habit: the most popular are low growing and stemless; the most dramatic have stout trunks.

PLANT TYPE Hardy, evergreen perennial or shrub

HEIGHT 16 in–6 ft 6 in (40 cm–2 m) in a pot, taller when in bloom

SPREAD 16 in–3 ft 3 in (40 cm–1 m) in a pot

POT SIZE One plant per 12 in- (30 cm-) diameter pot

CALENDAR

COLOR

LEAVES Blue-gray, often variegated

FLOWERS Cream

	WINTER	SPRING	SUMMER	FALL
IN LEAF				
IN FLOWER				

Yucca gloriosa is a large plant with spikes of magnificent creamy white flowers.

'Bright Edge' is a compact and colorful Spanish dagger, ideal for pots.

CHOOSE

The leaves of this plant add drama to any display; its flowers are a beautiful bonus. *Yucca filamentosa* and *Y. flaccida* are low-growing with flower stems up to 3 ft 3 in (1 m) high. They are hardy and suckering in habit, forming loose clumps of soft foliage. *Y. filamentosa* 'Bright Edge' has leaves margined with pale yellow, while 'Golden Sword' has leaves with yellow centers. *Y. gloriosa* is a far taller plant with thick trunks and thick leaves—these have sharp points and care must be taken in a patio to avoid injury. The variegated form is most attractive.

PERFECT PARTNERS Yucca leaves are always striking, but mix especially well with large, tropical plants. **LARGE** *Canna, Cordyline australis, Pseudopanax lessonii* **MEDIUM** *Aeonium arboreum, Melianthus major, Phormium* **SMALL** *Dianthus, Festuca glauca, Osteospermum*

PLANT

Yuccas are often sold as large plants and are best planted in spring or summer so they are established and have filled the pot with roots by winter. Plant in enriched potting mix.

Deep pots are best for *Y. gloriosa*, which can be top-heavy when fully grown. The top of pots is often filled with gravel for decoration, but bear in mind that this makes it difficult to see if the potting mix is moist, even though yuccas can withstand periodic drought.

GROW

Spanish daggers grow slowly but should live for years. Their biggest foe is wet soil in winter. Keep plants moist; feed once a fortnight in summer and fall. They will need repotting every two or three years. Slow growth and shorter than usual leaves are signs that plants need repotting or more feeding.

MAINTAIN The yuccas mentioned here are all hardy but can be damaged if the potting mix freezes. Insulating the pot from frost will protect the plants (see p.33). When the rosettes of the smaller kinds flower they slowly die, so they should then be cut out at the base.

INDEX

Bold text indicates a main entry for the subject.

Author Geoff Stebbings

PUBLISHER ACKNOWLEDGMENTS

DK would like to thank Oreolu Grillo and Sophie State for early spread development for the series, John Tullock for consulting, and Margaret McCormack for indexing.

PICTURE CREDITS

The publisher would like to thank the following for their kind permission to reproduce their photographs:

Alamy Stock Photo: Plantography 2c; PURPLE MARBLES GARDEN 8cl; Avalon/Photoshot License 8br; tom viggars 10b; BIOSPHOTO 11b; Avalon/Photoshot License 13tc; Debu55y 17br; Ros Crosland 22br; Zena Elea 28tr; Deborah Vernon 29cr; Parinya Yodchompoo 36tr; Premaphotos 36bl; Rex May 37bc; Nigel Cattlin 37br; 38c; Rodger Tamblyn 44bl; blickwinkel 45cr; Jonathan ORourke 49cr; blickwinkel 50bl; Fotografiecor.nl 50tr; RF Company 51bl; 52c; Jinny Goodman 54bl; Nigel Cattlin 55c; Avalon/Photoshot License 55br; blickwinkel 56cl; Bob Gibbons 59cl; Anne Gilbert 60tr; PURPLE MARBLES GARDEN 61tr; Barrie Sheerman 62bl; David Bratley 64c; John Glover 66tr; MusicMan5Photos 67cl; Dimitris Dimitris 67br; FlowerStock 68br; Robert Smith 68br; David Grimwade 69c; WILDLIFE GmbH 71tr; FLPA 72br; Aliaksandr Baiduk 73tr; blickwinkel 74bl; GardenPhotos.com 76c; John Richmond 78tr; Zoonar GmbH 83br; Dorling Kindersley ltd 85cr; Exotic and Botanical - Chris Ridley 86br; Julian Nieman 87c; Gary K Smith 87br; Selfwood 89cl; Plantography 90c; RM Floral 92bl; Ian Grainger 92tr; mauritius images GmbH 93cl; GKSFlorapics 94bl; Botany vision 98bl; Malcolm Haines 100tr; Matt Perrin / Stockimo 101tr; Tim Gainey 104c; John Richmond 106bl; Anne Gilbert 106br; F-Stop boy 108bl; Panther Media GmbH 108br; Anna Anisimova 111bl; Martin Hughes-Jones 114tr; RM Floral 118br; Steffen Hauser / botanikfoto 119cl; NorthernExposure 119br; Elizabeth Leyden 123tr; Elizabeth Whiting & Associates 124bl; Peter Turner 125tr; Holmes Garden Photos 127tr; Jane Tregelles 132cl.

Dorling Kindersley: Brian North 8tr.

GAP Photos: Nicola Stocken 9c; Andrea Jones 15t; Abigail Rex 23br; Nova Photo Graphik 49cl; Ron Evans 60bl; Nova Photo Graphik 71bl; Visions 75cl; Richard Bloom 81cl; Lee Avison 88br; Friedrich Strauss 95tr; Jonathan Buckley 102br; Nicola Stocken 107tr; Friedrich Strauss 115cr; Friedrich Strauss 127cl; Friedrich Strauss 131bl; Jonathan Buckley TBC 133cl; Jerry Harpur - Design Geoffrey Whiten 133tr; Friedrich Strauss 135cr; Nova Photo Graphik 139cl.

Geoff Stebbings: 40tr; 58bl; 70tr; 93br; 99tr.

Getty Images: fotografixx 16b; ermingut 47cl; steve wanstall 48bl; hphimagelibrary 66bl; AKIsPalette 73bl; Frank Sommariva 79tr; peplow 85cl; aansuu 95cl; lovelypeace 97cl; Michel VIARD 103tr; Yippa 110cl; P_PHOTO 112bl; berkay 113cl.

Huw Richards: 24bl.

Cover images: Front: GAP Photos: Juliette Wade

Illustrations by Cobalt id.

All other images © Dorling Kindersley

Produced for DK by COBALT ID

Managing Editor Marek Walisiewicz
Editor Diana Loxley
Managing Art Editor Paul Reid
Art Editor Roger Walton

DK LONDON

Project Editor Amy Slack
US Editor Megan Douglass
Managing Editor Ruth O'Rourke
Managing Art Editor Christine Keilty
Production Editor David Almond
Production Controller Stephanie McConnell
Jacket Designer Nicola Powling
Jacket Co-ordinator Lucy Philpott
Art Director Maxine Pedliham
Publishers Mary-Clare Jerram, Katie Cowan

First American Edition, 2021
Published in the United States by DK Publishing
1450 Broadway, Suite 801, New York, NY 10018

A catalog record for this book
is available from the Library of Congress.
ISBN 978-0-7440-2681-8

DK books are available at special discounts when purchased in bulk for sales promotions, premiums, fund-raising, or educational use. For details, contact:
DK Publishing Special Markets,
1450 Broadway, Suite 801, New York, NY 10018
SpecialSales@dk.com

Printed and bound in China

For the curious
www.dk.com